THE HEALTH & BEAUTY

HANDBOOK

THE HEALTH & BEAUTY

HANDBOOK

PAT BAIKIE

CHANCELLOR
PRESS

Previously published in 1988 by
Octopus Books Limited
part of Reed International Books
under the titles
Beauty Care and *Exercise and Diet*

This 1992 omnibus edition published by
Chancellor Press
Michelin House
81 Fulham Road
London SW3 6RB

© Reed International Books Limited
1981, 1984
ISBN 1 85152 125 9
Printed in Hong Kong

CONTENTS

INTRODUCTION

This book is for you if you care about your appearance but don't want to become a slave to your looks. You must admit that, taken too seriously, the whole business of beauty can become a time-consuming chore. Looking beautiful should be fun! The secret is to put minimum effort into producing maximum rewards. One way of achieving that goal is to let your natural assets and basic beauty routines work to your best advantage.

Take eating, for instance. Aim to eat for beauty and you will discover the delights of a slender figure and healthy hair, skin, eyes and nails. With positive assets like these, you can keep skin care and make-up in perspective.

Understand your skin - its type, how to treat it and get the best from it. Apply the same rule to your hair. Your skin maxim will be a minimum of maintenance, using preparations geared to your skin type. Don't expect miracles from pots and tubes - they're to make you look more attractive, not to create unnatural beauty.

A good figure can be more of an asset than a pretty face. It can be arresting and expressive, and is the first thing people notice from a distance. Apart from measurements in appealing proportions, what makes a figure attractive is suppleness, grace and pride of bearing. Diet and exercise are the key contributors. Literally everyone - fat, thin or just right - needs exercise. And whether you are fat or thin can be regulated by what you eat. If you wish to lose weight, your daily food intake must be reduced to supply fewer calories than you need; in that way you will use up the reserve energy you carry about in each surplus pound.

Beauty is a state of mind. Obviously good bone structure, make-up and beauty aids help, but in the main beauty comes from inside - from a feeling of well-being, a zest for life. If you feel good you will look good.

The Health and Beauty Handbook provides you with all you need to know about looking great and keeping trim and healthy.

PART ONE

BEAUTY CARE

SKIN CARE

SKIN CARE: FACE

Skin which has been looked after should be firm, yet elastic and full of glowing vitality. Maintaining that happy medium means keeping your skin scrupulously clean and balancing its care to suit every change – from the passing of years to the switch of seasons and temperatures.

Regular cleansing is tremendously important to healthy skin for we need to remove five types of dirt from our faces: perspiration, excess oil from the sebaceous glands, dust, dead cells and make-up.

Regular protection is necessary. Apart from actual bone structure, your face is made up of muscles, fat and the fluids which fill the tissues and give your face firmness and fullness. When you start to lose muscle mass or fat or fluid, wrinkles appear. This gradual loss of the skin's elasticity is a natural part of the ageing process and, although you cannot stop it, you can slow it down. A little prevention goes a long way towards warding off prematurely wrinkled skin. Proper cleansing helps, plus toning, moisturising and conditioning.

Your skin's needs vary with age. The pattern to expect is as follows. In your teens: normal/dry or oily/problem skin. In your twenties and thirties: normal/dry or oily skin. In your forties and fifties: normal/dry or dry skin. Sixties on: very dry.

From your twenties on, pay special attention to the delicate skin around the eyes – the most sensitive part of the face and especially prone to dryness and wrinkles. The throat area is vulnerable too, as is the neck – particularly prone to ageing because it has very few oil glands.

In any year, your skin may need to have its care adjusted. At home, in winter especially, both central heating and constantly varying room temperatures can make the skin feel dehydrated. This calls for more moisturising care.

Holidays at home or abroad can upset the skin. The weather, including sunlight, temperatures and humidity is generally to blame. From the skin's point of view, the most detrimental holiday climates are cold dry (mountain) air and hot dry (desert) air. In the former, you need to cleanse less frequently and apply moisturiser more often. In a hot, dry climate you are bound to perspire more which washes away the benefits of your moisturiser; you therefore need to apply it much more frequently.

Wherever the water is hard and contains chemicals, avoid soap and water cleansing; use a cleansing lotion instead.

How clean is clean enough?

No skin can ever be 100 per cent clean from one moment to the next, for the skin is constantly discharging a certain amount of sebum and perspiration to keep the moisture and oil balance within the inner skin. It's important that all the superficial debris is cleansed away regularly otherwise pores will become blocked and blemishes will start.

A really clean skin should have a uniform colour and translucency – free of debris to allow the upper layer to admit and reflect light. Since sebum flows at varying rates from different skins, an adequate cleansing routine for one skin may be far from sufficient for another. Every skin should be cleansed in the morning to remove the dead skin and oils discharged during the night, then again at bedtime and every time fresh make-up is applied. Frequency depends on the skin type; oily skin may need four or five cleansings a day.

Toning up

Tone or freshen your skin after you've cleansed it; this is an extension of cleansing. Choose an astringent lotion, skin freshener or toner: all help remove traces of make-up or oil from your skin. Most fresheners tighten the pores temporarily and stimulate circulation.

Adding moisture

Every type of skin needs a moisturiser to help retard the evaporation of natural moisture. Don't confuse the loss of moisture with the loss of oils; they are two different processes. Oily skins can lose moisture as well as oil and there are lightweight moisturisers for them. For oil-starved skins, there are heavier moisturisers which often add lubrication as well as moisture to help retain liquid in the skin.

Moisturising is an important part of any beauty routine, summer or winter. Your face is constantly exposed to elements which dry out the skin – sun, wind and cold weather, for example. Central heating creates a very dry atmosphere which can really upset natural moisture levels in the skin.

Your skin care routine

Normal skin: If you are fortunate enough to have normal skin, help keep it that way by using a cream or creamy lotion to cleanse it. At night follow this by washing your face with a mild soap. Tone your skin after cleansing with a non-drying skin freshener. Use a moisturiser at bedtime and under make-up – especially when the humidity is low.

Dry skin: Remove make-up at night with two applications of cream or a creamy lotion especially formulated for dry skin. You might also want to wash your face with a mild soap. Next step: tone your skin with a non-drying skin freshener. Since your skin needs plenty of lubrication, use an extra-rich cream at night, paying special attention to your throat and the area around your eyes. In the morning, wash with a gentle lather or – if you have very dry skin – rinse your face with warm water. Use a thin film of moisturiser under make-up at all times.

Oily skin: Wash with a cleanser – preferably medicated – in warm water at least three times a day; use a soap, liquid or gel cleanser. Massage with your fingertips, giving special attention to the forehead, nose, chin and hairline. Rinse off suds with warm water. Follow with a cold water rinse and pat dry. Sponge your face with cotton wool moistened with astringent or a non-oily medicated lotion.

Blackheads are usually associated with oily skin; they are caused by congestion below the surface. For treatment, see Skin problems (page 22).

Combination skin: If your skin is dry at the sides and oily down the middle, treat these areas separately – using dry skin preparations on outer areas and an oily-skin routine for the middle portion. It is perfectly possible to wash the oily part of your face more frequently than the dry areas. Massage cleanser on oily parts and rinse off with water using your cupped hand or a beaker.

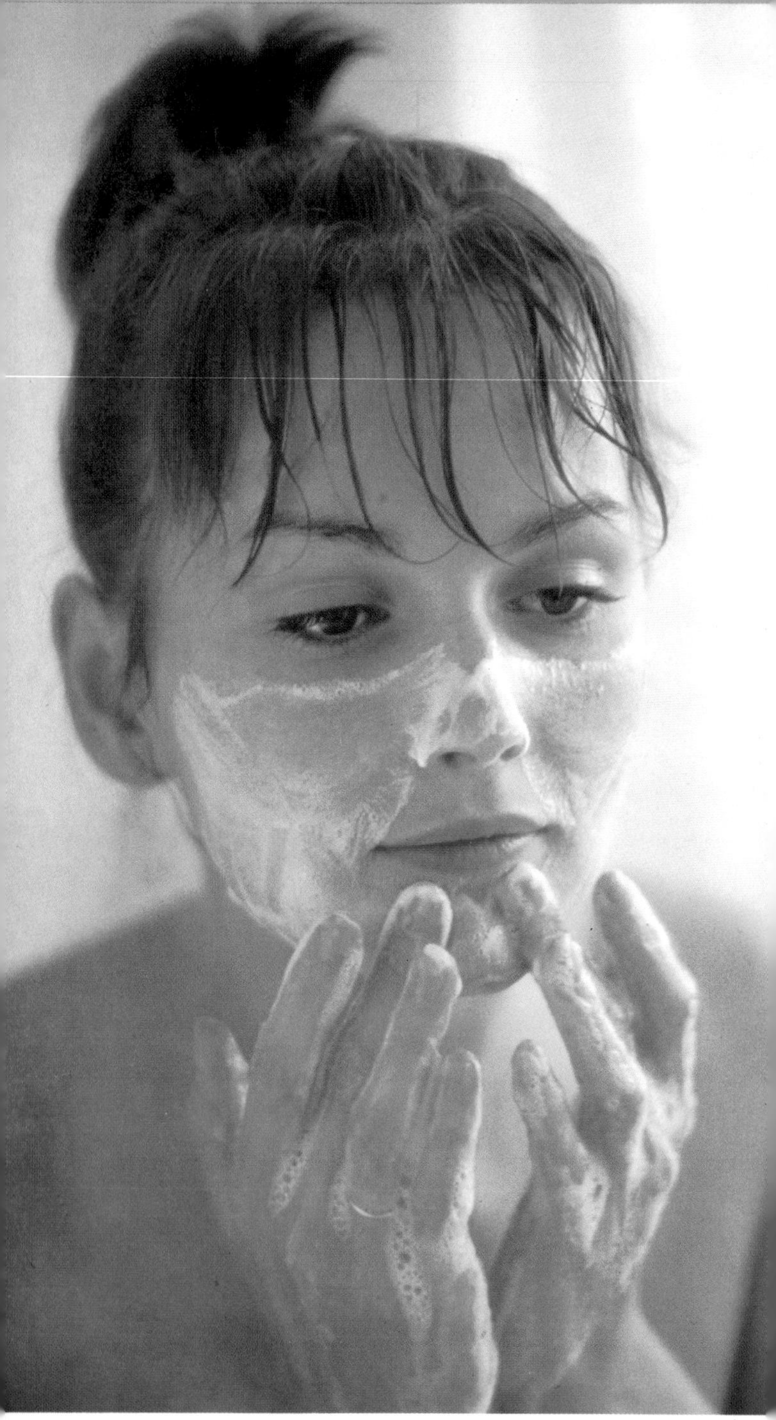

LEFT: *Face massage step 3. Making gentle circular movements on the end of the chin with the middle fingers of each hand.*

ABOVE LEFT: *Then working the fingers around the mouth towards the nose.*
ABOVE: *Smoothing fingers lightly over the cheekbones.*

Massage is 'exercise'

Massage, if performed correctly, brings a fresh supply of blood to the skin's surface, helps clear away impurities, feeds the tissues and tones up tired muscles. Aim to massage your skin once a week. You can use soap suds, moisturiser or a conditioning night cream. Massage for 5 minutes at a time. Always begin on the lower part of the face – working the cream or soap until it is soft and warm. Use six movements – all upward and outward – avoiding the area around the eyes.
1. Place left hand at the base of the throat and, with a firm circular movement, work up the right side of the neck towards the chin. Repeat, using the right hand up the left side of the neck. 2. With the backs of the hands slap briskly beneath the chin – one hand and then the other. Shake hands to prevent stiffness. 3. Place middle fingers of each hand on the point of the chin and make circular movements, working up round the mouth and in towards the nose. Smooth out lightly over the cheekbones. 4. Place middle fingers of one hand and then the other over cheek. Stroke briskly upwards using alternate hands. Repeat on the other side of your face. 5. Using both hands stroke up the centre of the nose between eyebrows and smooth out over brow towards the temples. 6. Then knuckle into the brow with rotary movements using alternate hands.

Handle with care

Care for your skin by handling it gently. Soaps, cleansing lotions and creams, moisturisers and conditioning creams should all be applied to the skin as gently as possible; otherwise you defeat the object of the application – which is to maintain youthful, supple and firm skin.

Never scrub or drag at your face. If you suspect that you are being heavy-handed, 'handicap' yourself. Instead of scooping up dollops of cream on your fingertips (wasteful, apart from anything else), use the middle finger only of each hand and learn to fingerprint products over the face instead of smearing them on indiscriminately.

Over the cheeks: When making-up, never try to apply cheek colour to a 'naked' skin. Moisturiser is a must if the colour is to go on smoothly and effectively.

RIGHT: *When you're wiping off cleansing cream or lotion, use a tissue to its best advantage. Instead of wasting several tissues – scrunching them up, one after another, and rubbing away at your face, try this.*

Wrap a tissue round your hand and fold over at the top to make a 'glove'. Wipe the tissue gently over the face. When one side is soiled, move the glove round to the clean side, then turn it inside out. Used in this way, one tissue can make a really smooth job of cleaning your face and help keep the texture firm at the same time.

Another tip – for quick, easy and gentle application of cleanser or freshener – make your own moist pads. Simply cut out circles of lint, pack them into a pretty, airtight jar and add enough of the product of your choice to saturate the 'circles'.

Around the eyes: When applying moisturiser or cream to the delicate skin beneath the eyes, use the middle or fourth finger of each hand. Look upwards and fingerprint the product on. Work outwards over the eyelids towards the outer corners, then inwards towards the nose. Finish with a series of small circular movements at the outer corner of each eye. If you are applying a camouflage product to dark circles or bags under the eyes, dot on the product and leave for a minute or two, until the warmth of the skin softens up the consistency; then blend it in with the fingertip. Alternatively, apply and blend with a brush.

On the neckline: When applying moisturiser or cream to the throat area, make sure that every single movement is upward and outward; this way you are lifting and firming the contours all the time.

Signs of the teens, twenties, thirties, forties . . .

Knowing how skin changes with age and being aware of the danger areas will help you work out your own individual skin conditioning routine. For this there are day and night moisturisers, conditioning creams for general facial application and, more specifically, for the areas around eyes and throat, and face masks.

Late-teens – early-twenties: A normal skin is smooth, soft and firm, with a clear, healthy colour. It can be compared with the unblemished, polished skin of an apple. Even at this age moisturising is important, as the natural moisture cells begin to deflate.

Mid-twenties: The ideal skin resembles that of a peach – more soft and smooth, less 'glowy' than an apple. Moisturiser helps counteract the appearance of fine expression lines around the eyes.

Mid-thirties: The average skin tends to become drier, loosing some of its elasticity and fresh colouring. The main areas to watch are around eyes and mouth. Fine criss-cross lines indicate dryness and really dry patches on cheeks or forehead show up reddish in colour. Remember: laughter is not the only emotion your face registers. You could also develop your share of frown and disapproval lines. The best

The skin around the eyes gives our age away more obviously than we like to think. Perhaps laughter is to blame, but try to keep lines and wrinkles at bay with gentle products and gentle handling of the skin.

defence is massage. At this age switch to richer day and night moisturisers and stimulate the skin with massage and moisturisers.

Early forties: Watch out for deepening of under-the-eye lines and a tendency for the neck to become drier. Continue the skin care pattern of the thirties and think in terms of 24-hour nourishment. Choose moisture-based make-up ranges and eye and neck creams.

Mid-forties and on: Without a good skin care routine, your skin will become extra dry and lax, with deeply etched lines around the mouth and eyes and on the forehead. Your skin could lose its natural colour and tiny surface capillaries could rupture, leaving small, purple-red blotches. Lax muscles can make the jaw-line heavier and the corners of the mouth might droop. The neck becomes more lined and the throat muscles sag a little. Gentle massage with appropriate creams can give good results in all these vulnerable areas. And remember that skin care need not only be a bedtime routine.

Skin problems

Allergies: If your complexion seems constantly itchy, chapped or very rough, you may be allergic to certain foods or cosmetics. Your doctor and/or a dermatologist can usually help you track down the cause. If cosmetics are the problem, you can minimise irritations by using hypo-allergenic creams and make-up. If in spite of that you still think a cosmetic you are using has triggered off a reaction, try to consider whether it is just an intolerance or insensitivity – a feeling of discomfort (eg wrong consistency) – rather than a real allergy.

Try a patch test. Dab the product on the inside of your wrist and wait 24 hours. If reddening or swelling occurs, you are probably allergic to an ingredient in the product and should stop using it.

Cosmetic ingredients that can damage the skin are either primary irritants or sensitisers. Primary irritants disturb the skin soon after application so they can be easily identified and avoided. However the allergic reaction to a sensitiser takes longer to develop – perhaps after weeks or months of trouble-free wearing of a product.

When you suspect you're allergic to something, write direct to the manufacturer concerned, returning the product and giving as much information as possible along the following lines. State when you used the product and whether you had used it before; describe the reaction, where it appeared and how soon after application; mention also any history of skin trouble. Manufacturers generally pass on complaints to the company chemist and/or consultant dermatologist who should come back with a satisfactory reply and alternative product suggestions. Most allergy complaints are resolved.

Blemishes: Minor skin problems can turn into more serious ones if they are not dealt with properly. If blemishes (blackheads and spots) persist in spite of careful skin care and good health, you should see your doctor. Blackheads are generally associated with oily skin and are caused by congestion below the skin's surface. Sebum in the skin becomes irritated by bacteria and a blockage occurs; when the head of the blockage meets the air it turns black, giving the blemishes their characteristic appearance.

Cleansing alone will not remove blackheads. Try softening them with hot compresses, then ease them out with a comedo extractor. This is a spoon-shaped instrument with a hole in the bowl through which you ease the blackhead or comedo – the medical term. If the number of blackheads increases, this may be a sign that oily skin is not getting clean enough and oil is building up to clog pores. Cleaning your face more often may help to prevent this build up.

Acne: This is a common complaint, especially among teen-agers. Acne is the result of a disturbance in the activity of the sebaceous glands – glands in the deeper layers of the skin which secrete fatty matter. While the exact cause of the disturbance is not known, both hormone imbalance and local bacterial infections seem to play a part in its development. Doctors suggest that emotional stress, fatigue, nervous tension, improper facial hygiene and certain foods, drugs and cosmetics tend to produce flare-ups of acne – though they are not causes. Acne can also be hereditary.

Although acne cannot be prevented, it can often be controlled once it appears, by following this daily treatment. First scrub your hands, then cleanse your face with a medicated soap, sudsy liquid or gel. Using your fingertips, gently massage lather all over face for a few minutes. Rinse with hot water, then with cool water. Do this three times a day, more often if you can.

If you see a pimple starting, apply a solution of equal parts of antiseptic lotion and water on a bit of cotton wool. Change to a fresh piece of cotton wool every 5 minutes and continue the application for about 30 minutes. Do this twice a day, after thorough cleansing. At bedtime and under make-up, you could apply medication, in the form of a flesh-tinted cream or invisible gel.

In addition to following this skin care routine, you should drink plenty of water and try not to become constipated. Wear an off-the-face hair-do to keep scalp oils and dandruff from drifting onto your face, and use a medicated shampoo often. If your skin problem is serious enough to require a doctor's care, he will probably give you a list of foods to avoid and procedures to follow.

SKIN CARE: BODY

The bath or shower is the best place for a beauty bonanza, taking in skin care over all. In the shower or bath, apart from cleaning your skin, you can do all the pumicing that's necessary. Water-softened hair is easier to shave and the warmth of the water makes the skin more receptive to lubrication. The lazy approach to achieving a good skin tone is to add a moisturising product to your bath or to use a body shampoo in the shower. If you don't add a skin softener to the bath water, then apply a good moisturiser-replacement lotion after a bath. Massage in the product until it disappears, not forgetting hands and feet. During or after a bath or shower treat specific problems.

Tiny pimples: Especially noticeable on the legs, but affecting arms and bottom as well, tiny hard spots are the direct result of bad circulation. The best cure is a daily circulation booster treatment in the form of massage. In your bath or shower, use a loofah, coarse bath mitt, pumice stone or stiff circulation brush and a good lathering soap. This treatment also helps remove dead cells. Then lubricate, using a good nourishing cream. Knuckle it in – working up from the ankles, all round the calves and thighs. Then smooth in hand and body lotion, until it is completely absorbed.

Rough, dry, scaly skin: This is usually most noticeable on the legs and is often the direct result of exposure to more extreme weather conditions. The ideal solution is to soak in a warm bath to which a few drops of oil have been added. Wash with a vegetable oil soap or use a bath additive instead of soap. When you use soap, make sure that it is rinsed off completely; soap residue can cause scaling. Dry yourself thoroughly, using a friction movement. Then massage the affected parts with a concentrated body oil.

Wrinkles: These always appear first on the face and hands, parts that are constantly exposed to the elements. Knees, armpits and between the breasts are also susceptible. Elbows wrinkle too, because of leaning pressures which dry the skin.

The gradual loss of the skin's elasticity which results in wrinkles is a natural part of the ageing process; unfortunately fair skin seems to age more quickly. You cannot stop wrinkles appearing but you can slow down the ageing process. After bathing and drying thoroughly, apply a body moisturising lotion, paying particular attention to the elbows and knees. Choose a body lotion to suit your skin type.

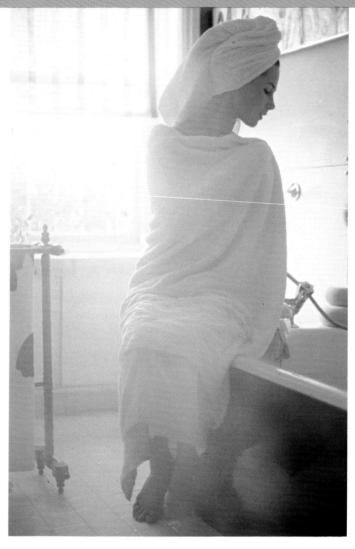

A MOCK SAUNA: *Use two large towels and ½–1 cupful of herbs; mint and chamomile blend well. Tie the herbs in one or two muslin bags.*

Make sure the windows and doors are tightly shut, then run the hottest·water you can bear into the bottom of the bath; suspend the herb bag under the pressure of the tap – to free the fragrance.

Soak the towels in the fragrant water and wring them out. Run more hot water and get up a good steam. Now wrap yourself, mummy-style, in the hot towels and sit on the edge of the bath.· When the towels cool off, remove them and relax in a heated room.

Bathing routines

A sauna bath: Sauna baths are becoming more popular. The first effect of a sauna is complete relaxation of body and mind. Through a lowering of blood pressure, mental strain often disappears and the muscles relax. The usual pattern is shower, sauna, shower, sauna and relax. According to the method of heating and the degree of humidity, the sauna can be a steam bath or a dry-heat bath. Perspiration usually starts after about 8 minutes, during the first sauna. After 10 to 20 minutes in the sauna, you take a quick shower, starting warm and getting gradually cooler. You then repeat the sauna session. Perspiration breaks out very quickly the second time. After this, you take a cold shower and then relax for at least 30 minutes.

By encouraging perspiration, a sauna helps to eliminate toxins and surplus waste from the tissues. Because of the water loss, you may experience a temporary weight loss after a sauna; this will disappear as soon as you eat and drink. Never stay in a sauna too long; this can cause over-fatigue and even fainting. Try a soothing mock sauna at home (see opposite.)

A relaxing daily bath: Aim to have a daily tepid bath (31–32°C/85–90°F), or a warm one (38°C/98–101°F). Soak for 10 minutes or so and blot yourself dry; don't rub your skin. Choose bath additives for their relaxing properties or make up your own herbal sachet, using dried herbs. Infuse by putting the herbs in a muslin bag and tying it to the hot tap so the water runs through the bag. A herbal bath soothes the nervous system, nourishes the skin and should include flowers as well as leaves. Two of the most relaxing and soothing herbs are lavender and marjoram.

A quickie bath: With only 10 minutes to spare before you must begin dressing again, run tepid water into the bath. Stretch out for 5 minutes, a wet face cloth over your eyes. Then scrub all over with a loofah and rinse off. Turn the shower attachment on you – as cold as you can take it. Rinse with tepid water. Towel-dry briskly to stimulate the circulation. Double the benefits of a quickie bath by using one of the bath salt preparations which contain mineral salts.

A speedy shower: The best value top-to-toe beauty treatment is to wash everything from hair down to toes in one easy session. Wash your hair in the shower and it becomes strictly a non-chore: no ricks in your neck, no damp necklines. With a couple of minutes to spare while hair conditioner 'takes', get busy with a loofah or sponge; go clockwise round your tummy to encourage the blood's circulation and keep your waistline trim. Rinse all over in tepid water, then give yourself a good rub with a coarse towel.

Always apply anti-perspirant deodorant first thing in the morning after washing. Make sure that you've rinsed off all soap traces; any residue can interfere with the remedial action.

Personal freshness

Personal freshness means more than a daily bath and a lavish use of fragrance. The real problem of overall personal freshness is that of dealing with body odour which emanates from the armpits in particular. Everybody perspires. There are approximately two million sweat glands all over the body. These work continuously even when no noticeable moisture is present. Perspiration is an important and necessary function of the body. Firstly, it helps your system to get rid of waste products. Secondly, as perspiration evaporates, it helps maintain normal body temperature by cooling your skin. Thirdly, because it is natural body moisture, it helps keep your skin smooth and pliable.

Odour only builds up when perspiration is in contact with the bacteria in the air for any length of time. Our faces perspire too, of course, but perspiration there is removed by relatively frequent cleansing. Obviously it is not possible to remove clothes and wash underarms with soap and water as often during the day. A deodorant is designed to counteract the odour of perspiration; an anti-perspirant is designed to inhibit the flow but it also contains deodorant properties. It makes sense to use one of the dual effect preparations.

Those who are anti anti-perspirants, either because they firmly maintain that 'sweating is natural', or because they believe that sealing off a few square inches stops the skin breathing, simply end up with damp stains on close-fitting sweaters and dresses. Total 100 per cent reduction of sweat is just not possible but anti-perspirants can reduce sweating considerably – certainly enough for comfort and to prevent clothes being marked.

Choosing your deodorant/anti-perspirant: Settle for a good functional aerosol, roll-on or cream. Roll-on anti-perspirant/deodorants are available in emulsion form and in a clear liquid which dries quickly and is less sticky. Whichever you choose, use it regularly – every 24 hours on average – and let the application set before attempting to dress. Aerosol sprays dry instantly; roll-ons and creams take longer. Most formulae are not water-fast and should be re-applied after a bath or swim.

Under-arm hair should be removed regularly as it can inhibit the effectiveness of an anti-perspirant deodorant. But what about the advisability of applying odour protection after hair removal? Most product instructions suggest waiting a few hours. An immediate post-shaving remedy is the application of a finely-milled deodorant talc.

A smooth finish

There are different ways of removing unwanted hair. Which works best for you is usually a matter of trial and error.

Electrolysis: This is the only permanent way of removing hair; the roots are killed by a small electric current passing through a fine needle. You relax in a chair while the operator treats the hairs. Fine hairs which have never been tampered with may disappear in one go, but most hairs reappear and need several treatments. Discomfort during treatment can be anything from a slight tingle to a short, sharp pain, depending on the sensitivity of your skin and the operator's skill.

Waxing: This treatment is effective for 3 to 6 weeks. Waxing rips out hair at the roots, with a double bonus: no dark shadow remains and regrowth is not usually stubbly. Many people avoid this method, not liking the thought of applying hot, wax and then ripping it off! In fact, the wax need only be warm; there are even cold applications for home use.

It's always advisable to have a salon wax first: partly because you study the expert's technique, partly because regrowth is consequently weaker and easier for you to deal with. Be prepared for post-wax tingle, especially in areas where strips have overlapped. Skin can also be tender and pink, so allow at least a day between waxing and a special occasion, or sunning.

Shaving: This technique cuts the hair across at skin level and stubble grows again quickly – in 1 to 4 days. You can 'wet' shave or use an electric razor. Ladies' razors are scaled to perform well under arms and around knees. With an electric razor, apply a pre-shave lotion first, or talcum powder which dries the skin thoroughly – to give a close shave. To wet shave, use warm water and soap (not shaving cream – the skin is too soft for that).

Depilatories: These chemical hair-removers, in cream, lotion or mousse consistency, give a smoother effect than shaving, with slightly longer-lasting results. For application, see below.

Tweezing: This lasts for 1 to 4 days and is fine for isolated hairs and eyebrows; it's not advisable for patches of hair. A disadvantage is that when a hair is pulled it often splits at the root and, with the next growth, two hairs appear in place of one. Tweezers come in ordinary-grip and scissor-grip styles with three types of tip: straight-across, diagonal and spoon-shaped. The straight-across tweezers seem to take a firmer hold on the hair; the diagonal ones cope better with obstinate stubble. Never pluck hairs growing from moles.

Bleaching: This technique is effective for up to 4 weeks and minimises the appearance of hair. A patch test is advisable.

LEFT: *Applying a depilatory. Always follow manufacturer's directions, which are generally along the following lines. Clean area with warm water, no soap. Apply depilatory with a spatula to a thickness of one-eighth of an inch; leave on for the recommended time. Try stroking first against the lie of the hairs, then with them. Most users wipe off the first application with a damp cloth and re-apply blobs of depilatory to stubborn hairs; after 2 to 3 minutes, these usually come away.*

31

First hand impressions

Of all beauty routines, the care of hands and feet has become the chore. This is a great pity when you think of the rewards, in terms of both comfort and appeal; the hands appeal to two senses – sight and touch. In some ways, hands are noticed as much as – and handled more than – faces; we wave goodbye, we shake hands with each other, we hold hands – and so on.

To keep hands supple: Spend a minute on massage at least once a day. Keep hands upright while working in the cream – to increase the blood flow from the fingers. Swivel the thumb on each hand, working in a dab of cream to each knuckle in turn; this helps enlarged knuckles and breaks down acid deposits. To loosen up fingers, massage the entire length of each finger in turn, from the base to the tip using the thumb and first finger of each hand (see above).

LEFT: *Removing 'old' polish before a manicure. Proceed as follows. Put a little remover in the middle of a swab of cotton wool. Then press the swab to the nail of the little finger. Wait a second or two and the polish will 'lift' cleanly away. Move on to the second nail and continue until you reach the thumb. Working from the smallest to the largest nail prevents smudging.*

LEFT: *Shaping nails. Use a long emery board rather than a metal nail file, it is more pliable and less likely to shred the nail. Never file away the sides or deep into the corners or you will damage the nail. Always file from side to centre.*
OPPOSITE PAGE: *Massaging fingers using the thumb and first finger of each hand.*

One of the best quick exercises to promote hand circulation is as follows: press and rub the hands vigorously from right to left, while rotating the wrists.

Caring for your nails: A nail takes approximately 16 weeks to grow from root to tip, so miraculous overnight cures for nails cannot happen. The best policy is to aim for trouble-free nails always – by manicuring 'little and often'. Always remove 'old' polish before a manicure (see above).

Weekly manicure routine: 1. File nails to a nice oval. **2.** Massage in cuticle cream. **3.** Soak nails for a few minutes in warm soapy water. **4.** Scrub gently with a nail-brush to remove dirt. **5.** Gently push back cuticles using a cuticle pusher, rubber end hoof stick or a manicure stick with the tip wrapped in a tiny piece of cotton wool. **6.** Apply nail varnish, if liked .

Foot-notes

Ill-fitting shoes are the cause of most foot problems; they can also be responsible for a bad back or poor posture. Corns, callouses and other localised thickenings of the skin are caused by pressure and friction which definitely start at shoe-level.

A well-fitting shoe should be half an inch longer than your foot and allow plenty of room for your toes to move. And the right size of tights or stockings is just as important; anything too small will cramp the foot and could cause, in the long run, bunions and hammer toes. When you are on holiday, give your feet as much rest from shoes as you can, and at other times walk barefoot around the house.

Bathing your feet: Aim to do this daily. Use warm, not hot water, and never steep your feet for too long – or you will dry out all the natural oils in the skin. When your feet are feeling 'achey', bathe them first in warm water, then in cold. Always dry your feet thoroughly, especially between the toes; moist skin can crack and this is how infections start.

Massaging: Using any left-over body lotion or moisturiser, or a special foot balm, massage your feet after every bath or shower. Massage in an upward direction, from toes to ankles, to stimulate the circulation. When your feet ache and there isn't time for a cold plunge, rub them briskly with cologne. If perspiration is a problem, spray on an anti-perspirant deodorant for feet; or splash on astringent, let it dry then dust your feet with talc.

Exercising your feet: At the end of the day, when you want to sit and relax, is a good time for this routine. Sit comfortably with your feet up on a chair and proceed:

1. Clench your toes, then relax them; do this six times. **2.** Stretch your toes and ankles, then 'pull them back' as far as you can – feel your heels pulling really hard. Do this six times. **3.** Draw circles in the air, moving the feet from the ankles; first one, then the other – six times clockwise each foot, six times anti-clockwise. **4.** Cross your feet, contract your calf and thigh muscles hard, then relax them. Do this six times. Then cross your feet the other way and repeat six times.

Pedicure: Aim to give yourself a pedicure once a fortnight. **1.** Soak your feet in warm soapy water, while you bathe or shower. **2.** Dry feet well, especially between the toes. **3.** Smooth rough spots by rubbing them gently with a pumice stone or abrasive lotion. **4.** Clip nails straight across using nail scissors or nail clippers. **5.** File edges smooth; don't file down into the sides of the nail because this encourages ingrown toenails. **6.** Push back cuticles using a cuticle pusher or rubber end hoof stick, or an orange stick with the tip wrapped in cotton wool. **7.** Apply nail polish if liked (see opposite).

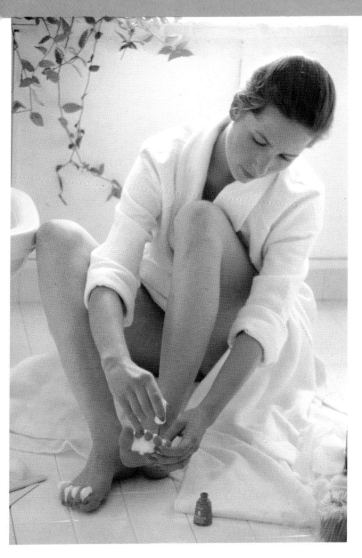

1. *Before applying nail polish make sure your nails are clean and soap-free. Wipe them over with remover.* **2.** *Brush on a base coat for smoothness and nail protection.* **3.** *Apply two coats of polish, using three strokes; brush down the centre of the nail first, then down each side. Wipe off a hairline of polish from each nail tip. Allow nails to dry for 5 minutes between each coat.* **4.** *Brush a colourless sealing coat over the nail and under the tip.* **5.** *Take off traces of polish on hands or feet with cotton wool soaked in remover. Separating toes with cotton wool blobs help to prevent smudging.*

35

A tan can take its toll

Apart from turning you brown, the sun can dry your skin and make it look older than it should be. Ideally, aim to get the colour right without ruining your skin. To achieve this tan sensibly, using adequate protection. You should also pre-condition your skin before going into the sun and always wear moisturiser – separately or as an integral part of a sun screen. If you apply ordinary make-up on sunny days, choose brands which contain sun filters. Equally important, never neglect after-sun care. All these points are vital if you don't want your skin to show signs of ageing before it should.

When normal skin is exposed to strong sunlight, it reacts very rapidly by turning red and eventually brown. What happens is that the melanin-pigment granules under the surface of the skin – are triggered off by the sun and migrate upwards. The ultimate depth of your tan depends on the amount of pigment your skin can produce. You will also reach a stage when your pigment is fully developed and you cannot then go any darker. With subsequent reasonable exposure, you can keep the colour topped up – that's all.

Care must be taken during the first few days of sunning. If you overdo this stage of acclimatization you risk getting sun-burned, and, in the long term getting toughened, and dried-out skin. Some people also make the mistake of not accepting their maximum tan and trying to achieve darker shades.

Actual sunburn is fairly superficial. Although it is painful it doesn't leave scars; only very occasionally, a few tiny broken veins may appear especially on cheeks and around nostrils. As far as ageing the skin is concerned, the sun is much more insidious. Remember that there are rays of two sorts: infra-red ones which provide heat, and ultra-violet rays in two strengths – long rays which don't do any harm, and short ones which do. For instance, if you expose yourself endlessly to the sun, ultra-violet will eventually penetrate through to the lower layers of the skin. This results in a break-up of those elastic tissues which keep the skin supple and youthful.

Equally harmful is moisture loss. When you have been swimming, especially in sea water, don't just dry off in the heat of the sun. Always towel yourself dry. Otherwise water left on the skin evaporates and that action has a magnetic effect, drawing out even more moisture from within the deeper layers of the skin itself.

In a nutshell, there's nothing like a tan for making you feel and look on top of the world, for a tan hides skin blemishes and contrasts well with teeth and the whites of the eyes. The way to avoid the pitfalls of tanning is to apply appropriate protection both during and after sunbathing.

MAKE-UP

MAKE-UP

Beauty is said to be in the eye of the beholder – and that's you, every time you look at yourself in the mirror and apply make-up. But there's more to making-up than meets the eye. How you see yourself and how you will appear to others can be quite different. Here's how to be sure of looking your best from any angle and in any situation.

Light up your looks: Always make-up in a light as near as possible to the light you are going to be seen in. For best daytime effect, your mirror should be backed up against the window which gets the best daylight; this way the light comes straight over the top of the mirror and on to your face. The Victorians and the Edwardians got it just right; that's why the 'ugly' backs of their dressing tables so often conspicuously occupied one of the front windows. If you want to avoid this situation, settle instead for a pretty table and a separate mirror.

To make-up for night time you ideally need about 250 watts lighting. It is best to have lighting along the sides and over the top of your mirror. If possible, position your table near a wall or ceiling light; a swivel spotlight is ideal, because you can direct the light over the top of the mirror – and place a table light either side of the mirror. If there's not much space, little half-shaded lamps are fine; turn the half shade to expose the light when you need it.

The minimum to do the maximum: This is the secret of a good make-up. Choose subtle consistencies and colours which don't conceal but simply highlight your natural good looks. It doesn't necessarily follow that the more natural the effect you are aiming for, the fewer products you need to use. You can use several and your face will keep the secret as long as you resolve to apply each product carefully, in a good light. And remember, the secret is to make-up – not patch up. In other words, be enthusiastic about make-up or leave it alone. Don't dab on little bits here and there. Patches of eye shadow on otherwise naked eyes, lipstick on a colourless face or blusher on a bare skin will only accentuate those areas of your face that are not made up.

Never make the mistake of slapping on foundation and nothing else in the forlorn hope that as long as you blot out the odd spot or blemish, you will get by without any other make-up. You won't. Foundation on its own looks flat and is very noticeable. It is worse than wearing no make-up at all.

Making up in your teens and twenties

Moisturiser is essential; ideally use a tinted one for a pretty, glowing 'canvas' which provides minimum coverage but maximum protection. Consider the best shades for your eye make-up. Brown is the most natural of all, with grey a close second. These colours may sound limiting but between the two there's a whole new colour spectrum you probably haven't investigated before: everything from soft freckle-browns to lovely deep, plummy mauve-greys. Most medium to olive skins already contain these pigments anyway, which is what makes them 'natural', but the tones are right for everyone, even a fair-skinned blonde. Ideally, blusher and lipstick should tone with eye make-up.

The bonus of linking complementary shades is that one product will very often do the work of two, or three. Take a brown eye pencil, for instance. Obviously, it's great for tidying up the shape of the eyebrows and – as long as the consistency is soft enough – for outlining eyes and lips too. Follow that with a brown eye shadow in the same tone as the pencil: blend over the eyelids, then fluff it on as a face shader.

An alternative approach to eye make-up is to use one powder eye shadow and apply it wet and dry for different effects. You'll need two brushes, of course. Use one to apply the shadow wet – as an eye liner; the consistency goes on two or three shades darker than it appears in the palette. Use the second brush to apply the shadow dry, as usual, over the eyelids. Then take a pink-tawny tone eye shadow and use that as a highlighter high on the lids under the eyebrows. The colour can also double up as a cheek blusher. This pink-tawny shade is just right for a blonde with blue eyes or a brunette with blue, grey or hazel eyes. If you have auburn hair, you need a more definite tawny shade.

So with three products, plus moisturiser, you can achieve a pretty flattering make-up. All that is missing is mascara; this is a must and, to go with this colour scheme, choose a dark brown one. Never let mascara give itself away by allowing the lashes to stick together so they become stiff and spiky. The secret is to use a wet brush or wand for application and a dry brush to take off any excess and to spread the lashes.

Finally, don't forget lipstick. A tinted lip gloss is the ideal consistency to team with a tinted moisturiser face base; keep heavier, deeper lipstick colours and textures for times when you are wearing a full make-up. Outline the lips first, then fill in with lip gloss. You really do get the most natural effect with a thin outline of dark colour filled in with a more translucent lip gloss. Here, a lovely old-rose pink tones in beautifully with the pinky-brick colour of the eye highlighter and blusher.

LEFT: *Without make-up.*
ABOVE: *After applying the minimum make-up for maximum effect. First thing in the morning, apply tinted moisturiser then eye make-up. Here a brown eye pencil is used for eye liner, eyebrow pencil and lip liner; brown mascara is brushed onto the lashes. Apply, then carry with you, two eye shadows, to reinforce cheek and eye colour. And lip gloss to give lips a lovely smooth sheen.*

43

Making up in your thirties and forties

All women, over a certain age, should wear a tinted foundation over moisturiser. Foundation not only helps even out a blotchy skin tone, it also acts as a 'canvas' for the rest of the make-up. Powder comes into its own now too, both the loose variety, to set foundation, and a compact of pressed powder for touching up during the day. Both should be colourless – usually called translucent. The golden rule is to match your foundation to your skin tone. Use powder as an invisible topping. It's folly to think you can blot out mistakes in foundation choice by dusting on lashings of coloured powder.

Around the age of forty, eyes start to need definition rather than heavy make-up. It is very important to keep eyebrows neat and tidy; regular tweezing is necessary. The rule is that the brow should start directly above the inner corner of the eye and stop at the point where a pencil slanted from the side of your nose past the outer corner of your eye meets the brow. Make sure the outer end of your brow is as high as the starting point and check that the highest point of the curve is immediately above the iris. If you are thinning the whole arch, always pluck from underneath, never above.

With definition in mind, you need a grey or brown pencil to outline eyelids, to help make lashes look thicker. Start at the top and draw a fine line, keeping as close to the base of the lashes as you can. You might find it easier to transfer the colour to a fine brush which can edge in really close to the lashes. Define under the eyes too, but not too much – just at the outer corners and in slightly, about one third of the way along; then blur the line with the fingertip.

Take an eye shadow, in much the same colour tone as the pencil. Use it to ring the crease of the eyelid, where the eyebrow bone meets the lid, and right round under the outer corner of the eye. Blur the line until it's hardly noticeable, then introduce the first vestige of real colour. Remember that browns and greys are for definition only. Use one shadow on the actual lid; another, if you like, as a highlighter right under the eyebrow. Be sure to blend in the colours where they meet, so there are no harsh outlines.

Mascara is the next step. Apply one coat sparingly with a moist applicator, then brush the lashes through using a dry brush.

Fluff blusher on cheeks and, with what's left on the brush, apply a touch of colour high up on the sides of the face – winging out from the eyes. This is the simplest and most effective 'face-lifting' trick there is. For the lips, an eye pencil can double as a lip liner. Outline the lips first, then fill in with lipstick, avoiding pale pinks and true orange colours.

44

LEFT: *Without make-up.*
ABOVE: *After applying the minimum make-up for maximum effect. In the morning, carefully apply foundation and loose powder, then eye make-up. Here a grey eye pencil, grey shadow over the eye lid, darker blue-grey on outer part of lid and cream highlighter on brow. Mascara and lipstick complete the effect. Take with you pressed powder, blusher and lipstick for touching up.*

45

Choosing and using foundation

A good foundation evens up your skin tone and helps to hide any trouble spots. Beige or cream tones help to tone down a florid skin. Pink tones emphasise a fair skin and add glowing colour to a sallow skin. Neutral beige tones give a delicate look and tone down a ruddy complexion. Beige tones are generally more flattering to older skins. Golden honey tones promote a healthy, outdoor glow. It is a mistake to try to alter your colouring too much with foundation – choose a colour within two shades lighter or darker than your skin tone.

Foundations are available in creams, cakes, gels and liquids. The texture of a foundation can help you achieve your ideal skin tone. A liquid foundation is ideal; it provides a light protective film with a fairly good coverage. The secret is to dot the liquid all over your face and neck and smooth in lightly with downward strokes. Blend quickly and carefully, especially around the hairline and jaw, making sure that the colour fades out with no obvious demarcation lines.

To find the shade that's best for you, compare the colour in the bottle or tube with the skin tone on the inside of your wrist or on your neck in daylight.

Using powder

Over half of the most common problems with make-up are caused by not wearing powder. This is invariably the reason why make-up disappears by 11 o'clock in the morning and why it becomes greasy-looking very quickly after application. Powder takes the shine off your face and gives skin a velvety finish as well. The best kind to use is translucent; colour should come from your foundation, not your powder. It is also easier to achieve the 'see through' look if you use a loose powder rather than a pressed one.

RIGHT: *Applying foundation. Dot on sparingly over your forehead, cheeks, nose and chin, then smooth in gently from hairline to jawline. Use your fingertips or a barely damp sponge to obtain a thin even film. Apply foundation over moisturiser and under powder for a lovely, lasting effect.*

To apply powder: In the mornings, pat loose powder on lightly with cotton wool or a powder puff over your foundation, then dust off the excess. Artists' brushes, the plump fluffy sable ones, are also ideal for applying powder. For the smoothest finish, always blend in powder using downward movements. This is the direction in which facial hair and down grow. If you stroke your face in the opposite direction, you will fluff up the fine hair and make it more visible.

To finish: After applying foundation and powder, for good measure, wring out a cotton wool ball in icy cold water and lightly pat it all over your face. This 'sets' the make-up and helps its 'staying power'.

Choosing and using face colour

Face blushers are a whole new category of colouring products which have evolved from rouge. To use blushers properly you must appreciate the principles of light and shade, then apply them to your face shape. The blusher family is made up of three different groups.

There are the natural looking peach and pinky tones which add colour to the cheek area. Shaders are the darker tawny, brick, rust and plum tones which literally help shade away specific areas. Highlighters, which are usually creamy luminous tones, do just the reverse and draw attention to certain areas. Difficulties usually arise when it is not appreciated that all three varieties shouldn't just be plonked on the cheeks. The pinks and peaches are right for the cheeks; they should be applied high on the cheekbone. Shader is more likely to go under the cheeks to create pretty 'hollows'. Highlighter is applied very high on the cheekbones – above the natural-looking shade.

Brush-on colour is applied after powder. Cream or liquid goes on before powder; use the dot and blend technique, rather as if you are applying foundation. Not sure where your cheekbones are? Find them with your fingertips. Then apply pink or peach 'cheek' colour lightly along the bone, blending

CORRECTING FACE SHAPES WITH BLUSHER

LEFT: *Round face. Apply 'natural' cheek colour along the cheekbone; shader to help minimise fullness around the chin.*

RIGHT: *Long face. Apply 'natural' cheek colour along, and highlighter above, the cheekbone; shade out the end of the nose and the chin.*

48

up and out towards your hairline. Don't blush too close to your nose or lower than the tip of it or you lose that 'lift.'

When you are feeling really tired, there are other 'face-lifting' tricks to try. Brush on colour lightly along the top of the forehead, under the chin and over the bridge of the nose. When it's your eyes that are looking weary, wing colour out to the temples and in again, just above the eyebrows.

Where to put shader and highlighter really depends on your face shape. If you're not sure what yours is, get another opinion and go on to master the technique of light and shade. For instance, a round face can take a dusting of shader to help minimise fullness in the chin, and doesn't usually need highlighter. A long face can take lots of highlighter, well back above the cheekbones to give an illusion of fullness and width. If your nose and chin are on the long side too, a little shader applied to the end of each can make them appear shorter. A square face can take shader well down towards the jaw and highlighter fluffed really high on the cheekbones, to widen the upper part of the face. A triangular-shaped face can take a lot of highlighter both sides of the forehead and a dusting of shader from the ear lobes, fading out at the chin.

Whatever the shape of your face, check that you haven't created an unnatural effect by applying too much blusher.

LEFT: *Square face. Apply 'natural' cheek colour along, and highlight above the cheekbone and shade down towards the jaw.*

RIGHT: *Triangular face. Apply 'natural' cheek colour along the cheekbone, shader on the sides of the face, highlighter on the edges of your forehead.*

Choosing and using eye make-up

Aim to build up a wardrobe of eye colours and wear two or three at a time in different combinations. One suggestion is the blue/primrose eye (see right); you will find more colour schemes on pages 54 and 55. The secret of blending two or three colours successfully is to let them overlap to avoid hard edges. Powder shadows are easily applied and blended; so are creams – but be sure to blend the crease-resistant variety quickly because they dry soon after application. If you are over 35, choose matt textures rather than irridescent ones for the actual eyelid; wear irridescence as a highlighter under the brow bone. Powder shadows stay in place better when applied to lids which have been slightly moisturised.

If you have less-than-perfect eyes you need to use neutral contouring shades; the correct shades used in the right places before you apply your actual eye colour scheme can make problems disappear. To identify your eye type, see Correcting eye shapes.

Apart from eye shadow, you will probably want to apply pencil liner and mascara. A soft eye pencil makes the eyes seem larger and the lashes thicker. Draw a thin line along the base of the upper lashes, then outline the lower lashes from the centre of the lid outwards. If you don't like the idea of a continuous line, use pencil to dot on colour between the lashes and you will still achieve the lash-thickening effect. Blend the line, if you like, with your fingertip or blur the edge with a fine brush.

Another reason for wearing eyeliner is to give your eyes a more expressive shape. When this is your intention, start the line at the inner corner of the eye and widen it a bit towards the centre, thinning out again at the outer corner. It's a good rule to match the colour of your eye pencil to that of your eye shadow or mascara.

When you stroke on mascara, be sure to coat lashes all the way to the tips. For a lavish look, coat the tops first, then brush up from underneath to curve lashes slightly. When the mascara has dried, separate the lashes with a clean dry brush or wand. As a colour guide: brunettes should wear black mascara; blondes and fair redheads, brown or charcoal; everyone else should use dark brown.

You may need to shape and colour your brows with eyebrow pencil. If the colour is right, you can also use the pencil for outlining eyes and lips. Never draw on one hard line and don't colour the actual skin if there is a hair you can pull into line instead. For the best light-handed approach, curve the heel of your hand around the cheekbone and draw in the shape with light flicks from the wrist.

THE BLUE/PRIMROSE EYE
BELOW: *Outline lids with
blue-grey pencil and blend
darker blue shadow over and
beyond the pencil line.*

ABOVE: *Use brown pencil on
eyelid crease and outer corner.*
TOP: *Dust pale lemon shadow
all over eye. Then apply
mascara and touch up with
blue-grey pencil.*

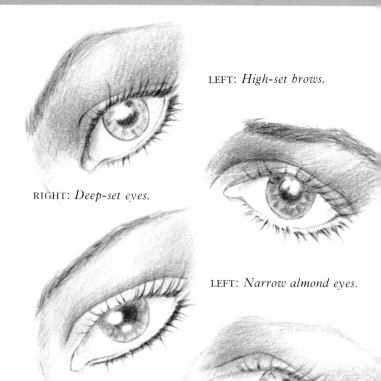

LEFT: *High-set brows.*

RIGHT: *Deep-set eyes.*

LEFT: *Narrow almond eyes.*

RIGHT: *Wide-set eyes.*

Correcting eye shapes

By using light and dark neutral eye shadows and pencil, it is possible to correct any eye shape problem. You must do this after putting on foundation and before going on to apply your actual eye colour scheme.

High-set brows: To underplay the lid area and minimise the space between brows and eyes, apply a pale shadow, such as mauve, from lashes to brows, then use a grey pencil to outline the eyes.

Deep-set eyes: A 'wash' of brick-coloured shadow from lashes to brows 'reduces' the eyebrow bones. An irridescent pearl grey pencil emphasises lashes, which helps bring the eyes forward.

Narrow almond eyes: A gold colour, blended from lashes to brows, highlights eyes. A grey line along the eyelid crease is also needed. Use a black pencil to outline lower lashes and create an illusion of depth.

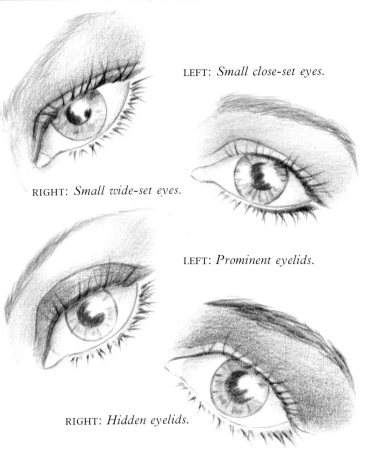

LEFT: *Small close-set eyes.*

RIGHT: *Small wide-set eyes.*

LEFT: *Prominent eyelids.*

RIGHT: *Hidden eyelids.*

Wide-set eyes: A frosted grey shadow, on the lids and smoothed high into the corners, helps draw eyes closer together. A darker grey pencil used to partially outline the lids helps to define the eyes; outline top and bottom lids, working from the outer corner and fading out as you reach the centre.

Small close-set eyes: Light brown shadow from lashes to brows 'widens' the lids. Use a dark liner just at the inner and outer corners.

Small wide-set eyes: Moss green smoothed on the lids and high into the corners brings eyes together. A black outline around the outer corners helps to define and enlarge the eyes.

Prominent eyelids: To make the lids seem to recede, apply a wash of brown shadow, from lashes to crease line; play up the area above with beige highlighter. Use brown eye liner.

Hidden eyelids: Reverse the technique for prominent lids: apply beige shadow to the eyelid area, and brown shadow above – up to brows. Draw the thinnest eye line possible.

Eye catching colours

Almost any colour scheme goes as long as the colours are subtly applied and blended.

For dark eyes: One of the most effective colour schemes is the mauve/brown eye (see above). Apply deep mauve shadow all over the lid, with beige-brown as a highlighter under the brow. Outline the eye with a grey-brown shade.

Also for dark eyes, consider a combination of pink/blue. Apply rose shadow on the lid, grey-blue shadow to emphasise the outer half of the lid, and dark grey as a liner.

There is also the grey/copper scheme for dark eyes. Apply silvery-grey shadow all over the lid, a touch of copper shadow in the centre of the lid, and use dark grey to outline.

For grey eyes: Try a mixture of brick/plum colours. Apply the brick tone all over the lid and use the plum shadow to emphasise centre of lid. Use a tawny brown pencil to outline.

54

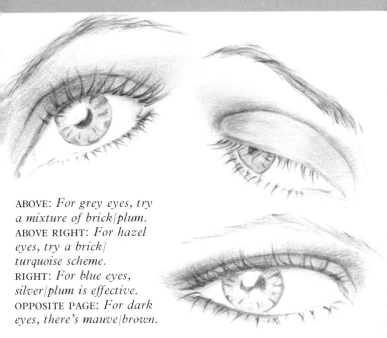

ABOVE: *For grey eyes, try a mixture of brick/plum.*
ABOVE RIGHT: *For hazel eyes, try a brick/turquoise scheme.*
RIGHT: *For blue eyes, silver/plum is effective.*
OPPOSITE PAGE: *For dark eyes, there's mauve/brown.*

A brick/green colour scheme also works well for grey eyes. Apply pale brick shadow to the whole eye area, then use a dark green shadow on the lid and a dark green pencil to outline.

For really dark grey eyes, there is the mauve/pink eye. Use mauve shadow on the lid, pale pink as a highlighter under the brow and dark grey, or even black, to outline.

For blue eyes: A silver/plum colour combination is really effective. Apply plum shadow over the lid, then dust over with silver. Use silver-grey to outline – the darker the better.

Also for blue eyes is the grey/brick combination. Shade the whole lid with brick and cover with grey. To outline, use grey.

For a true blue scheme, apply pale blue over the whole eye area. Use darker blue on the outer half of the lid and a similar shade for outlining the eye. Put a touch of cream highlighter shadow into the extreme inner corner of the lid.

For hazel eyes: There is the brick/turquoise combination, Use pale brick shadow on the inner half of the lid, turquoise on the outer half. Use tawny brown to outline.

Beige/grey gives a lovely sophisticated subtlety to hazel eyes. Apply grey-gold shadow all over the eye area, then grey shadow to the lid. Use green to outline.

Primrose/green is pretty. Dust primrose shadow on inner half of lid, moss green on outer half. Use dark green to outline.

For green eyes: There is the brick/gold scheme. Apply pale gold shadow over the whole eye area, then dust brick over the lid only; use tawny amber to outline.

Choosing and using lipsticks

Eye make-up and lipstick go together. Wear one without the other and your face will look out of balance. A brush or a lip liner pencil is almost essential, if you want to emphasise the shape of your mouth. And it's a good idea to outline with a strong colour, deep pink, plum or brick, then fill in with a paler frosted shade. This technique gives a lovely luminous effect. (See opposite: a tawny brick outlines lips, a pale brick is used to colour them in.) As a general rule, blot frosted lipsticks, but not matt ones. And, for touching up during the day, carry lip gloss with you; it is a mistake to keep piling on more and more lipstick.

Unless you are really expert with make-up, it's not a good idea to start tampering with the shape of your lips by blotting out with foundation and drawing in new outlines. The clever approach is to use colour to create the illusion of a different shape. This method is less time-consuming and likely to be much more successful.

Full lips: To condense this shape, choose a clear, bright colour. Always apply lip gloss before you stroke on the colour. Lipstick applied over a gloss doesn't appear as dark and has a sheerer texture.

Ill-matched lips: Often lips don't match each other in size. The top lip is thinner and smaller than the bottom. One lip colour over-all just exaggerates this, so it is a good idea to use two different shades, both in the same colour spectrum, but one slightly deeper than the other. Use the deeper shade on the top lip.

Thin lips: Warm amber to brick tones are best for this lip shape. Outline thin lips with a deep tone, then fill in with a paler frosted shade.

CORRECTING LIP SHAPES

ABOVE: *Full lips.*   ABOVE: *Ill-matched lips.*

ABOVE: *Thin lips.*

ABOVE: *For a perfect lipline, start by steadying your hand. Prop your elbow on the dressing table or let your chin support your little finger. Relax your mouth.*

Whether you're using a pencil or a lipbrush, carefully outline the bow first, then draw in the corners and connect with a straight line. Gradually build up the lower lip curve. Then fill in with lipstick or again, if you prefer, a brush.

57

Correcting face faults

By using colour carefully, you can do a great deal towards correcting any facial irregularities. Your palette is the whole beige to brown spectrum, taking in everything from very pale to quite dark shades and including all sorts of consistencies: tinted moisturiser, foundation, powder, sticks of concealer make-up, specialist camouflage preparations, face blushers, shaders and highlighters, and eye shadows.

The golden rule is this: any part of your face you want to make smaller make darker; anything you want to emphasise, make lighter.

For bags under the eyes: Use a foundation one shade darker than the foundation you are using all over your face and brush it precisely on the bag, in a thin line; it should be crescent-shaped.

For dark rings under the eyes: Use a pale make-up concealer stick or foundation one shade paler than the one you are applying elsewhere. Alternatively, a white or cream eye shadow highlighter, which is too pale to be worn on its own here, is effective when applied under foundation.

For noses of all shapes and sizes: Slim a nose by putting dark foundation down the sides, blending well at the edges. Make a nose look straighter by applying a light line down the centre; use foundation or pale concealer stick and blend well. Shorten a nose by putting dark foundation right under the tip and blending in well.

For nose to mouth lines: Use a light make-up concealer stick. Transfer the product onto a brush and trace a fine line along the groove; this is the same technique as the one used for bags under the eyes.

For a mouth that sags at the corners: Use a brush to apply a touch of light concealer stick to the area.

For freckles: The right foundation is helpful if you want to hide freckles. Choose a shade that's a little darker than your skin tone and a little lighter than your freckles. Follow it with pressed powder in the shade closest to your skin tone. If you have some particularly giant freckles you can cover them up with an opaque make-up. Freckles are intensified by the pigmentation which comes from the sun and certain climatic conditions. In summer, when you are probably leaving off make-up anyway, you might prefer to even out the freckle areas – especially on the cheeks – by fluffing on a tawny face shader which merges well with freckle patterns.

For more serious skin blemishes and scars: Use special masking and toning creams which help camouflage. These are of a more dense texture and are more heavily pigmented than ordinary make-up. If they are applied carefully, in the right

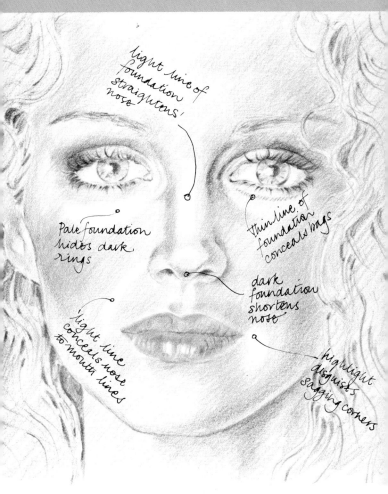

light line of foundation straightens nose

Pale foundation hides dark rings

thin line of foundation conceals bags

dark foundation shortens nose

light line conceals nose to mouth lines

highlight disguises sagging corners

combination of shades, these cosmetics are practically indistinguishable on the skin.

For high colouring: Apply a beige-toned foundation then set with loose powder; this should provide sufficient camouflage. High colouring is usually concentrated on the cheeks and around the nostrils. It stems from tiny cracks just beneath the surface of the skin into which traces of blood can escape. Fine sensitive skins are particularly prone to these thread veins. If the condition is quite serious and foundation and powder doesn't provide effective cover, consider a tinted moisturiser with a slight green cast to counteract the floridity; you can then go on to apply foundation and powder as usual.

For moles: Make up your mind whether you are going to tone down the odd mole with special masking make-up or make the most of it as a beauty spot.

Special considerations for the over-fifties

Over a certain age you don't make-up you 'make down', which simply means that the older the skin, the more fragile it becomes and the less make-up it needs. This doesn't impose any restrictions on the number of items used, but it does mean that it is more important than ever before to apply them lightly and subtly for maximum effect and minimum coverage. Remember when you apply make-up that the 'canvas' is wearing thin.

Learn to warm your foundation in the palm of your hand; cold application drags the skin. And fight the temptation to put on too much foundation, especially around the eye area; the skin here almost inevitably darkens in colour with age. The secret is to have two shades of foundation; one to go all over, a lighter one for the area under the eyes.

Most women give up powder after a certain age, but it is not necessary to do so. Powder is still the best way to set make-up for the day. Get the better of wrinkles by gripping the powder puff or a pad of cotton wool between forefinger and thumb, then hold the skin taut and press powder down onto the skin with a light 'heeling' movement. Always dust off any excess; it's important to avoid a powdered look – that's very ageing.

There's a lot you can do to 'lift' your face with colour. Eyes tend to narrow as they get older, so use a pale eye-shadow colour – preferably not blue. Use this as a wash over the whole eye area, blending up and outwards towards the temples; remember that lines that go up look younger than lines that droop. Green eye shadow is a good choice; it suits most skin and eye colourings. Use a pale green for the lids, then edge along the lashes with a darker green, blurring the application with the fingertip. For staying power on the lids, mix powder

LEFT: *Without make-up.*
RIGHT: *After applying the minimum of make-up for maximum effect. Foundation and powder together are essential. Delicate toning shadows are ideal for eyes. In this case green; pale green as background and a darker moss shade to emphasize the base of the lashes. One light coat of mascara is flattering too. Make sure that your blusher and lipstick tone for the best effect.*

shadow with a little moisturiser and apply carefully.

Be very careful with mascara – apply one coat only. Powder lashes first if you want to make them look thicker. Avoid using black; there are lovely greys and browns which will suit you better.

A touch of blusher makes the face look younger. For the right place to put it, feel with your fingers where your cheekbone starts below the temple. Blend in the colour along the bone, pushing up slightly against it. Don't apply blusher above your cheekbones or too near your nose and avoid a downward line; finish with a flick upwards.

One of the best ways to arrive at the right consistency and colour of blusher is to mix a little of your lipstick colour choice with moisturiser or cold cream. To team with green eye make-up, warm rust is ideal.

Special effects for the bride and mother

For most brides, making up to wearing white means a completely new approach to beauty. The effect of an all-white or cream wedding dress and veil is to create an aura which seems to suffuse the face and transform complexion colour. Girls who are not in the habit of wearing anything pale or pastel-toned might well find that their usual make-up needs playing up or playing down. This also applies to the bridesmaids or the bride's mum – if she's wearing something paler than she would normally choose.

The first essential for the leading ladies in the wedding group is a flattering shade of foundation. If your dress is dazzling white and the bridesmaids' or mother's choice green, blue or lemon, choose a foundation one shade warmer than the one you usually wear. If your dress is a warm cream, with pink or gold for bridesmaids or mum, consider foundations one shade paler than usual.

Skin texture should present no problems, if you plan wedding day looks far in advance and eat sensibly for a slim figure, shining hair, glossy nails and a clear skin. Just in case excitement produces an isolated spot on the actual day, match a medicated camouflage stick to your foundation colour. To encourage your make-up to last all day, apply translucent loose powder over your foundation. And carry with you a compact of translucent pressed powder for touching up your make-up occasionally throughout the day with no build-up of colour.

Blusher is the most important part of wedding day make-up. Choose rose-pink or subdued amber shades to emphasise the cheekbones and forget about reds and plums – these come out far too dark in photographs. A pale and pretty irridescent blusher always looks good fluffed on to the brow and winging out from the cheekbones – to emphasise the eyes; this gives a shimmering effect to the make-up and 'rebuffs' any shadows cast by the veil.

For photographs, the paler the eye-shadow, the more noticeable your eyes. This doesn't mean that you are restricted to green or blue. Try pale amber, warm beige or cool lavender. Choose grey liner and mascara if you are brunette, brown colours if you are blonde. Ideally, wear one pale shadow all over the lid; use brown or grey in the crease line and to outline the upper and lower lids. Don't over-do the mascara.

For lips, choose a medium tone lipstick in the same colour spectrum as your blusher. And either mix the lipstick with lip gloss or apply gloss on top of your lip colour, for a beautiful luminous effect.

ABOVE: *The bride wears a paler foundation than usual and translucent loose powder; a matching compact is to hand. She needs two blushers – one for cheeks and a paler version to fluff on forehead and tops of cheeks. Eye make-up consists of shadow, pencil to emphasize crease line and lashes, and mascara.*

Lipstick is topped with gloss.

The bride's mum is wearing a cream blouse, so the same rule applies for a cool foundation and translucent powder. Because her coat and hat are blue, she needs a more vibrant pink blusher and a blue-pink lipstick tone. Her eye make-up is grey-blue.

PARTY EYES IN CLOSE-UP
LEFT: *For a brunette –*
sparkling blue shadow on lid,
pearly highlighter on brow-
bone; brown along crease.
RIGHT: *For a blonde –*
there's glittery pink on the
lids and creamy highlighter
up to the brow-bone.

Special effects for a party

Choose colours that glow: Candle light or any subdued lighting is very flattering but gives little light. To be seen at your best avoid dark foundations or muted tones; your skin tone should be clear and light-reflectant, so that your face glows. Choose clear colours for eyes, lips and cheeks; muddy in-between shades just don't look as good in night light as they do during the day.

Try textures that gleam: Several kinds of make-up now come with glitter added, as well as in their regular form. There are foundations with a touch of shimmer, frosted lipsticks and lip glosses, and irridescent face powders, eye shadows, cheek blushers, shaders and highlighters. And, with the possible exception of lipstick, any one of these items can double up in all sorts of ways – highlighting temples, the crest of the cheekbones, the shoulders even. The purpose of all these products is to light up your face, but they can also make you look frostbitten or garish if applied with too heavy a hand. Girls still in their teens can get away with wearing everything in the glitter spectrum at once. Over-twenties need to wear it more subtly by combining carefully chosen glitter with their normal make-up to create a lovely glamorous effect. Here are two foolproof ways of applying glitter effectively.

Party effects for brunettes: The colour scheme illustrated above (left) is particularly good. To achieve this look, apply your usual foundation and powder, then dust on a frosted cheek blusher. Use one or two of the lightly frosted brush-on eye shadows and slick a frosty gloss over your lipstick. Choose vibrant pink for both lipstick and cheek colour. Sparkling blue is the shade for the eyelids, with brown accentuating the eyelid crease and winging right round the outer corner of the eye. Shimmering cream highlighter plays up the eyebrow bone.

   Remember it's important to choose clear colours for lips, eyes and cheeks; as long as all these areas are equally bright, the results look good. It's only when the balance of colour is wrong that the whole effect can look overdone.

Party effects for blondes: Here's how to achieve the stunningly attractive scheme illustrated above (right). Apply make-up just as you usually do. Then fluff translucent powder, in a gold-fleck, silver or opalescent shade, all over your face (except your nose – shimmer here looks too much like shine). Pink is the colour to use for eyes, cheeks and lips. Keeping to one colour tone, like this, is the way to achieve a really luminous make-up. Pink is good with a blue or black outfit; gingery tones are best for a green or yellow outfit.

HAIR CARE

HAIR CARE

Nature determines the texture, natural bend and growth rate of your hair. The rest is up to you and depends largely on how – and how often – you use hairbrush, shampoo, conditioning cream and other aids to gloriously healthy hair.

Of course, all sorts of conditions can affect hair health and, as always, prevention is easier than cure. Generally, if you eat to keep your skin healthy, you will find your hair is healthy too. From then on, correct care will help maintain the hair and scalp in a healthy state.

Brushing
Aim to brush your hair every day. Brushing stimulates the flow of blood to the scalp, removes dirt and debris from the hair and helps spread sebum, which is produced at the base of the hair, along the hair shaft. Brushing smooths down the scales of the cuticle, the outer layer of each hair, and gives a glossy sheen. It also helps to subdue 'static'. All hair types benefit from brushing.

Choosing your hairbrush: The correct brush shape for your hair will depend on its texture; i.e. fine, average or coarse. The right bristle consistency will depend upon whether your hair is thick, average or thin. For coarse hair, use a semi-radial shape – one with a 'half-moon' of bristles. For average hair, try a complete radial brush – one with bristles all round. If you have fine hair, choose a paddle (flat) shape or a radial brush. For thick hair, a mixture of nylon and bristle is best. An all-bristle brush is good for thin hair.

How to brush: Always brush (or comb, for that matter) from the roots of the hair to the ends. And always brush your hair dry – never wet. Brushing wet hair can cause cuticle damage which results in split ends. Brush before shampooing to distribute the natural oils right through the hair.

If you have long hair, use two brushes rather than one. Put your head down and brush from the nape down towards the ends of the hair, to coax much more volume into your hair. As you brush, you will find that the bristles penetrate more and more easily until you are touching the scalp each time with the bristles. Don't hack at your hair and don't flatten it down to your head; lift it in wide curves. Brush as rapidly as you like but don't flick the brushes harshly when you reach the ends of your hair. Finally, bring your head up again and brush down from the top of your scalp.

Shampooing

Shampooing the hair cleanses it and makes it springy and fragrant. Choose your shampoo according to the condition of your scalp.

A dry scalp feels 'tight' and can become so tense that headaches result. Over-shampooing can remove all trace of natural oil. Try diluting shampoo with water before applying it to hair.

With a greasy scalp, the skin is quite pliable – you can move your scalp under your hand. For this scalp type, use warm, not hot, water and give an extra final rinse.

A normal scalp looks healthy and has a good, normal skin colour. If your scalp is normal, concentrate on it more than your hair with the first application of shampoo. With the second, massage suds into the bulk of the hair.

With a dandruff-prone scalp which visibly sheds scales, make sure you rinse off every speck of shampoo and wash combs and brushes at the same time.

How often should you shampoo? As often as is necessary for your kind of scalp – once a week certainly, but perhaps as frequently as every day. As long as you are using the right shampoo, you needn't worry, either about drying out your scalp, or encouraging a greasy scalp to become more oily.

The shampoo drill: 1. First brush out all tangles; brushing also removes loose dirt and dandruff. **2.** Massage your entire scalp, briskly but gently, with a rotating movement of hands and fingertips. **3.** Wet your hair all over with warm water and either spot shampoo all over the whole scalp, or pour shampoo into the palm of your hand and apply it to the hair. **4.** Lather well and massage the shampoo well into your scalp with the same massage movement – a rotation of hands and fingertips (not nails). On this first application, concentrate mostly on shampooing the scalp rather than the hair; your scalp needs laundering most. **5.** Rinse off with warm water. **6.** Lather again and repeat massaging movement, paying special attention to the area around the hairline where make-up and debris can collect. Then rub the ends of your hair between your palms carefully with suds. *Note*: If you are washing your hair almost every day this second application of shampoo is not usually necessary. Equally, if your scalp is very greasy you might prefer to stick at one shampoo; over-enthusiastic shampooing can stimulate the sebaceous glands to produce more oil. **7.** Rinse the entire head thoroughly. Rinse and rinse again until you are absolutely certain all soap is rinsed away. A shower attachment giving a constant flow of water is ideal for this; you can just continue rinsing until the water runs clear. Any shampoo not rinsed away will have a dulling effect on your hair. **8.** Finish with a cold water rinse to give your hair more shine and gloss, then squeeze gently to remove excess water. At this stage, you may want to apply conditioner (see page 64). **9.** Blot your hair with a towel. Never rub too fiercely; apart from the danger of damaging the hair, you can also stir up the sebaceous glands to renewed activity – something to avoid, if your scalp is inclined to be greasy. **10.** Go on to dry your hair immediately, or wrap it in a towel, turban-style for a few minutes. The towel will absorb all the moisture and when you unwind it, your hair will be at the damp-dry stage.

BELOW: *Massaging the shampoo well into the scalp with the fingertips, using a brisk rotating movement of the hands (step 4, the shampoo drill).*

Massage

Massage is marvellous for easing a tight dry scalp. It also activates the tiny oil glands at the base of each hair, encouraging them to lubricate each hair shaft just enough for elasticity and 'bounce'.

Dry-massage: Work over your scalp in three easy stages. **1.** Start at the nape of the neck and work towards the crown. Use your thumbs only to begin with and pay particular attention to the whole neck area because that's where tension is most likely to build up; you should be able to feel any little knots of tension. Leave your thumbs in position at the nape of the neck until you have reached the crown with your fingertips; work in circular movements and use the pads of the fingers – never dig in with the nails. **2.** Now work from the temples up to the crown, placing hands either side of your head, with thumbs braced to support the fingers. Manipulate the scalp with the pads of the fingers, as before. **3.** Now concentrate on the area around the hairline which really benefits from massage because the skin here is very fine and the supply of natural nourishment less good. Equally, this is the area where make-up and debris collect; massage helps to get rid of any build-up.

Wet-massage: This method is performed with hair conditioner, prior to shampooing. It helps stimulate hair growth – especially when the hair has been badly damaged through over-exposure to the elements. To wet-massage, start at the nape of the neck with the fingers spread out, and travel slowly towards the crown, moving the scalp with kneading movements. Repeat from the temples and forehead.

OPPOSITE: *Dry Massage. Work from the nape of the neck up to the crown.*
BELOW: *Then massage from the temples to the crown.*

BELOW: *Finally concentrate on the fine skin around the hairline, which particularly benefits from massage, as it receives little nourishment.*

ABOVE: *Combing conditioner gently through hair to ensure even distribution (step 2, conditioning routine).*

Conditioning

Choose conditioner for the state of your hair – which isn't the same as the state of your scalp. The most normal hair conditions are as follows. 1. Dry unmanageable hair usually has a fuzzy outline and often goes with dry scalp and coarse hair. 2. Lank, dull hair frequently goes with a greasy or dandruff-prone scalp and average to coarse hair. 3. Splitting, or brittle ends often go with a normal scalp and occur in all hair-texture types.

For dry dull or brittle hair, conditioner is a must. It coats the hair and makes it smooth and shiny. Conditioned hair no longer feels rough and it has extra fullness and body. Lank dull hair needs conditioning too – to give it body. There are totally oil-free conditioners which are ideal for this hair type. Even if your hair is normal, make a concentrated effort to massage conditioner onto the hair ends; by doing so you can often help prevent injury to the hair shaft with the inevitable outcome – split ends. When these occur, the ends of the hair literally open up like a 'Y' and a split can travel right up the hair, leaving a series of broken wisps all over the head.

Remember conditioner is the invisible 'raincoat' which will help any hair type stand up to bad weather. Curly hair swells up and becomes difficult to handle in damp weather; conditioner helps curb this tendency. Long fine hair goes limp at the first sign of dampness; conditioner adds body. Fine wavy hair goes wispy; conditioner helps keep it smooth.

Conditioner is normally applied after shampooing. It will close any open cuticle scales and replace the natural oils which protect the hair. Left on the hair for a minute or two, a conditioner acts as a detangler and adds shine, body and lustre to the hair. Apply conditioner once the hair has been thoroughly rinsed after shampooing. Never massage conditioner into the scalp. Usually, you will only need to apply conditioner from the middle to the ends of the hair; the roots don't normally need it unless the hair is bleached.

The conditioning routine: 1. Pour conditioner into the palm of the hand, then gently squeeze onto the hair. **2.** Comb the conditioner through the hair to ensure an even spread. If the comb doesn't slide through easily, don't tug at the hair. Rather hold the jet of water from the spray head behind the comb and let the force of the water mix with the conditioner and smooth the path for the comb. **3.** Leave conditioner on for a minute or two before rinsing hair thoroughly with warm water. **4.** If your hair is very dry, reapply conditioner to the ends, about the last 5 cm (2 inches), and then rinse lightly. **5.** Blot dry with a towel or wrap the hair in a towel-turban which will absorb excess moisture. Never rub at the hair with a towel after conditioning or you will undo all the good work of the conditioner.

Deep-conditioning formulae: These are for use regularly once a month, or every six weeks, or for times when the hair has become badly damaged through over-exposure to wind or sunshine, sea water or chlorinated water. For this routine: **1.** Massage your scalp, working up warmth. **2.** Part the hair four ways and smooth conditioner onto each part, starting at the roots if the hair there is showing signs of damage; otherwise begin half-way down the hair shaft. **3.** Wrap your hair in a towel turban and leave your hair for at least 20 minutes. **4.** Shampoo your hair in the usual way.

Choosing your style

Thinking of changing your hairstyle? Then don't ask more of
your hair than it can possibly give. For instance, thin limp hair
will never look good in an elaborate arrangement; coarse curly
hair cannot be persuaded to give a smooth bob effect. Apart
from the texture of your hair, other considerations are the
shape of your face, your features and general proportions.
Healthiest hair is always shortish hair because it never gets
long enough and old enough to be damaged. Long hair can be
healthy if it's looked after well and trimmed regularly.

One length hair, blunt cut: See above. The important thing
to remember with this style is that hair never grows evenly all
over the scalp – so you can't keep a clean shape-holding edge
unless it's scissor-cut regularly. Every six weeks to two
months is just about right. Don't persevere with this style if
your hair is very fine and gets greasy quickly or if it tends to
split.

If you are into your thirties and still clinging to the
shoulder-length style of your teens, maybe it's time to think
again. Wear your hair like this if it's in good condition, and
you have a good forehead and hairline; if necessary you can
camouflage an uneven hairline by selecting tiny wisps and
trimming them short.

LEFT: *One length, blunt cut for medium to long hair. A band keeps hair off the face.*

ABOVE: *A slightly graduated bob cut; the hair brushed off the face at the sides.*

This length of hair can also be plaited or braided, or worn up in a French pleat or a top knot. Braid it before going to bed and you will have a gently rippled effect when you comb out the next morning. For quicker 'sets', you can brush and blow dry or use pin curls. But with this amount of hair you must pin curl the hair damp and not remove the pins until the hair is completely dry; otherwise the weight of the damp hair will make all the curl drop out.

A bob shape, slightly graduated: See above. This is a very versatile style and absolutely right for anyone growing out a fringe. Brush the hair slightly away from the face at the sides and it's good for all face shapes, except those that are long. Brush it back and away from the face at the sides and it has a really slimming effect on a round or heavy face.

After shampooing, to coax maximum volume into this style, brush and blow dry the hair with the head down. Then, when your hair is completely dry, throw your head back and double brush for maximum shine and manageability. This step is particularly important if your hair is fine.

Short, layered hair: See above. This style is ideal for anyone with fine hair and plenty of it. Naturally curly hair is also very suitable. You can brush and blow dry it for a flat, sleek effect, or make it extra curly with rollers or curling tongs, then finger dry it – just to trace the pattern of the natural movement in the hair. This style flatters heart-shaped and oval faces but isn't so good for a round face. It can work for a square face, if the hair is combed in the right direction; i.e. into soft rounded lines, waving over the brow and with enough fullness on top to detract from the width of the forehead and chin. The style is also good for a long face, providing you keep the sides full and the ends flicked up.

Hair as short as this needs to be trimmed regularly; every four to five weeks is ideal. And in just one trim or cut, short hair lends itself to a complete change of style. Clever scissoring means hair can be persuaded to fall forwards instead of backwards, or swept to one side or the other. Short hair really is versatile – in a way that long hair never can be.

A word of warning: if you are undecided about having your hair cut short or very short, before you do anything, take a sharp look at yourself in a full-length mirror and ask yourself this question. Are you planning to perch a gamin haircut on a large frame? Remember for the best overall effect your hairdo

LEFT: *A short layered cut, made extra curly by styling with curling tongs.*

RIGHT: *Medium length, layered hairstyle, ideal for fine hair.*

should be in proportion to the rest of you. Similarly, a mass of wavy long hair can overpower a petite figure. Make up your mind before you are sitting in the hairdresser's chair. Always give a new style long and careful thought before you book an appointment for a drastic change.

Medium-length hair, very layered: See above. This style is marvellous for fine hair; layering it like this gives it much more interest. The fringe is also very layered to give a flattering effect. This style combines the advantages of short and long hair, without being too conservative.

Layered hair suits most people because it's very good for softening any hard lines or features. Furthermore, because the shape is so versatile, you can play with it to suit any face shape. If you have a hard jaw or a square face, curl the side pieces onto the face to soften the angularity. Dry this style with your fingers for nice natural movement. Curl it all over, or tong the edges, or pop in heated rollers – for a soft face-framing effect. For an unusual variation, put the back up in a French pleat and go on to curl the front using tongs or rollers.

Drying and styling

Finger-drying: You can put a lot of shape and bounce into short layered hair by lifting and drying with the fingers. Towel dry to blot up excess moisture. It is important to have your hair at the damp-dry stage before you begin finger-drying. If you begin when your hair is very wet, it will take much longer and the extra handling can mean that by the time your hair is dry it's also quite greasy.

Start off by simply running your fingers through your hair. Finger-drying is exactly the same technique as double brushing – but you are using your hands instead of brushes. Generally work in the direction in which you want the hair to go. For an off-the-face short, layered effect, work the hair away from the face all the time with upward movements, one hand following the other. And, on reaching the middle length and ends, keep turning the hands over to obtain a slightly curled effect at the ends.

Brush and blow drying: This is a quick and easy way of introducing shine and bounce into the hair. The secret is to

BELOW LEFT: *Finger-drying a short layered style, working the hair away from the face.*

BELOW RIGHT: *Brush and blow drying long hair, lifting the hair to speed the drying.*

have the hair at the damp-dry stage before you start. So after shampooing, comb all the tangles out of the hair, and blot dry with a towel. Ideally, leave your hair wrapped in the towel, turban-style, until you are ready to start blow drying.

The hair-do that blow dries most successfully of all is an absolutely perfect blunt cut. Your hand dryer shouldn't be too cumbersome to hold. Check that its speed is right for the effect you wish to achieve; a minimum of 900 watts is best for random blow drying.

With the brush in one hand, dryer in the other, concentrate on putting volume into the roots of the hair. Pull and stretch, section by section, and follow through the length of the hair, keeping the direction of the hot air going from root to end. Keep lifting the hair, to speed the drying process.

Or, as an alternative method, forget all about going along carefully, section by section. With your brush, wrap the hair around the head and brush round in the opposite direction to the final fall of the hair; this way you can coax a lot more volume into the roots.

Avoid over-drying your hair. When you reach the just-dry stage, run your hands through the hair. The slight amount of natural oil on your hands will help to prevent static building up and create a better shine.

Rollers and pin curl sets: Rollers come in all shapes and sizes. Use them to wet-set the hair or to dry-set it. If you are dry-setting, use heated rollers, lightweight plastic ones or the sponge variety. The size of rollers is important; those with a diameter of 3.5 cm (1½ inches), give a smooth effect and body to the hair. If your hair is limp or you want more curl, use smaller rollers. If you want your hair to wave rather than curl, twist each section of hair first and then wrap around the roller so that the hair unwinds in a spiral.

You will get the best results from a roller set if you part hair neatly and make each section no wider than the length of the roller and no deeper than the diameter of the roller. Comb each section of hair in the opposite direction from the way you will wind it: straight up for rollers that turn down at sides and back, straight forward for rollers that turn back over the top and crown.

Make sure the ends of your hair are smooth and flat against the roller before you wind it; if the very ends get hooked up, like a crochet hook, the final result is an uneven hairline. One

BELOW: *Dry-setting medium length hair. Large light rollers are used to achieve a flattering soft wavy style. Smaller ones are used at the sides – to obtain more curl.*

way to avoid this, especially with heated rollers, is to wrap a tissue round the roller, before placing it in your hair. Fasten each roller directly over the part of your scalp the hair wound around it grows. Fasten rollers securely so they won't sag as your hair dries. You might try clipping each roller to the one below. For added body, apply a little hair spray.

If you are wet-setting your hair, dry off excess moisture before putting in rollers. If possible, let your hair dry naturally, or use a hooded hairdryer. Do not try to speed up drying by holding a dryer too close to your head.

How to turn a pin curl: Pin curls make pretty fluffs of curls. Just as rollers placed in dry hair give a 'booster' set, so pin curls can put more spring into wispy tendrils around the hairline, on the forehead and at the sides of the face. When used to set wet hair, pin curls make really resilient curls. They will also set wisps of hair too short to go round rollers. And they can add body to a roller set when a single row is used above and behind the ears at the nape of the neck.

To make a perfect pin curl, take your section of hair, pop a tiny piece of cotton wool on the ends to keep them smooth and, starting at the centre of the strand, wind the end around your finger. Slide the coiled curl off your finger and turn in towards your scalp. Fasten with a pin curl clip.

BELOW: *For a professional pin-curl style take time to wind pincurls correctly. The secret is to wind in every stray hair before pinning.*

Curling tongs: These are suitable for any length of hair, whatever the style. They are used for adding fullness to the hair, curling and straightening, or for creating waves. Tongs are used mainly for adding a little more movement to your set immediately after blow drying; or for boosting a set in between shampoos – they are especially useful if you have greasy hair which 'drops' its set from one day to the next.

The basic technique is to part the hair into sections that are no more than 5 cm (2 inches) square, and to work on one section at a time. To prevent the ends of the hair from buckling, carefully wrap a tissue round them before you start to tong.

To coax maximum fullness and volume into the hair: Wind the whole head of hair in towards the scalp, section by section; leave in rolls all over the head until the hair has cooled down. By the time you finish rolling the last section the first will have cooled. Don't be tempted to brush or comb out your hair too quickly; you could finish with a frizzy style instead of beautifully shiny and controllable bounce.

To curl hair under: Start with the hair underneath. To do this, you should ideally pin the bulk of the hair out of the way; gradually unpinning it section by section. Start at the roots and smooth each section in the tongs; as you get towards the ends, curl the hair slightly. Do not 'roll' the entire length of the hair.

To wave hair: Place the tongs near the roots of each section. Then wrap the hair around the tongs, winding right to the very ends. Hold for 30 seconds. Unwind and leave in a ringlet to cool down. When you are waving with tongs, it is especially important to be careful about sectioning off the head tidily; this way you can get as near to the roots as you should. With haphazard and careless sectioning off, you will end up with 'sausage curls' starting half-way down the section of hair, instead of ringlets which spring from the scalp and comb out into waves that are full of movement and resilience. Unless you wind from the roots, the tongs can leave an imprint on the hair – where the movement starts – making it obvious that your waves are anything but natural.

If you intend to use curling tongs regularly, it is a good idea to apply an after-shampoo protein conditioner, as a pre-ventative, just in case over-enthusiastic tonging has a drying effect on your hair.

ABOVE RIGHT: *Curling hair under, starting at the roots and smoothing down the length of each section.*

BELOW RIGHT: *Waving hair, wrapping each section round the tongs and winding right to the ends.*

ABOVE: *Help with hennaing.*
A friend, wearing protective
gloves, applies the henna to
the hair section by section.

Colouring and perming

Many hands make light work of perming or hair colouring.
The problems of coping alone with a home perm or a hair
colourant are twofold. In the first place, you can't see your
head from every angle, even with a three-sided mirror.
Secondly, just think how your arms ache if you have to hold
them over your head for any length of time. So it definitely
helps to have someone else carrying out the instructions for
you. This is especially true with a home perm, as you can't
wind the rollers properly at the back of the head yourself; also
with a hair colourant which is applied to the hair section by
section – it's impossible to make really regular partings in your

own scalp. Help with the hennaing process is most valuable because it is rather a messy procedure. Henna is a natural vegetable dye from the dried leaves of an Egyptian privet. It comes in a powder form, which is mixed with boiling water to a paste – resembling green mud.

For real success with hair colour, narrow down the vast selection of shades available to those that suit your skin tone. Nature usually gives us complementary hair and face tones, but the match is very often low-key. Altering your hair shade simply intensifies the colour scheme and makes it high key.

The secret is to choose a colour that is no more than three shades darker than your natural colour and no more than four shades lighter. So if you are naturally blonde, you can lighten to ash tones or darken to really warm golden and honey shades. If you are naturally mousey, you can lighten to blonde or darken to rich honey, tawny brown or subdued-red. If you are naturally a redhead, you can lighten to a honey blonde shade – never an ash one – or darken to browny-chestnut or reddish-copper. If you are naturally dark brown, you can lighten to golden brown or honey blonde or deepen your colour to include glowing red highlights. If you are naturally grey, you can lighten to a pretty, highlighted grey or darken to a natural-looking brown.

How long will the colour last? As long as you want it to. Shampoo-in colourants vary from permanent and semi-permanent tints to temporary colourings which last from one shampoo to the next (and the next shampoo could be within a matter of hours if for some reason you don't like the effect). Henna is becoming more and more popular for anyone wanting colour and improved condition for their hair. Whichever method of hair colouring you choose, it's important to follow instructions to the letter – and that includes patch testing for possible allergy.

Perming is a much-maligned process simply because, in the old days, so much could – and often did – go wrong. But today's perms are designed to give special body to the hair and styling flexibility without odour or the fear of frizzing. Perming works by softening the structure of the hair and rearranging it in a curved or curled pattern. It's the way you wind the curl that sets the pattern of your perm. This is why it definitely helps to have a friend on hand to check that the hair is divided into neat sections and that the tissue-covered ends of each strand are wound neatly around the perm roller; a neutralizing agent then sets the hair in its new shape.

The technique for straightening hair is much the same as the process for perming it – but in reverse. A similar process is used, but the hair is straightened – rather than curled.

PART TWO

DIET AND EXERCISE

SELF
ASSESSMENT

SELF ASSESSMENT

Body Image

The immediate impression of the kind of person you are is made by the way you look. Instant 'You' is visual, more potent than a thousand words and, rightly or wrongly, people will rate you accordingly. If your appearance is trim and pleasing, you begin with an advantage in dozens of situations – college interviews, job interviews, standing for office in club or class. There's some justice in this superficial appraisal, too: the care you take of yourself is an authentic indication of your self-esteem, an appreciation of your own worth. Don't confuse it with vanity, for they are very different.

What do you really know about yourself? If you have ever listened in wide-eyed wonder to a recording of your own voice, you know how difficult it can be to recognize the way you sound to the outside world. The same difficulty exists in recognizing the way you look to other people. You never see yourself from the back or in motion unless you have been taught to observe yourself as a singer, actress, dancer or fashion model does. Women tend to concentrate on their faces in a mirror as though their heads were disembodied. A sudden accidental glimpse of the whole figure reflected in passing a shop window or caught in a candid snapshot can sometimes be rather a shock.

Given that the time has come to take stock of your assets and of those things which can and should be improved, where do you start? At home, with time to spare, aim to make a cool appraisal that is neither rose-tinted nor deprecating. Do it wearing undies in front of a full-length mirror in a good strong light – and make notes. Examine your figure front and profile. Check the posture of your normal stance when at ease. Note all your good points, the things that need work and those problems which you simply cannot change.

No matter how grim your final list looks you ought to feel encouraged – you have actually begun to do something about it. Forget what you can't change – like your bone structure, the length of your neck or legs. Make up your mind to work on the 'improvables' and approach the task realistically. The degree of effort involved depends on the scope of the problems you want to solve. For instance, losing a lot of weight or correcting serious figure problems requires an energetic long-term programme and patience, whereas adjusting posture can be accomplished in minutes.

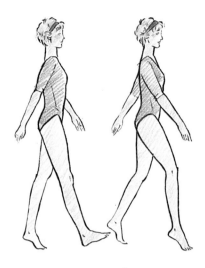

WALKING WELL: Step out on a straight leg. Point your foot directly ahead and come down on your heel, then shift weight to the ball of your foot. Keep head up, arms swinging easily, your step springy and alive.

STANDING TALL: Stand one foot turned out a little, the other a bit ahead. Keep back straight, knees relaxed, hands at your sides. Your tummy and buttocks should be tucked in, your chest up, chin parallel to the floor.

Posture

Like the expression of your eyes or mouth, your carriage is a key to character. Standing and moving well signals self-confidence as well as grace. Are you upstanding, with straight shoulders, pulled-up rib cage, tucked-in tummy, a trim bottom and naturally flexed knees? When you sit down, can you fit both hands – flat, one above the other – between your bosom and your waist? If you can't, you're too crumpled up.

Now stand with your back against a wall, feet about 7.5 cm (3 inches) from it. If your posture is close to perfect, your head, shoulders and buttocks will be touching the wall; the small of your back won't be more than a hand's thickness away. Check your profile in a full-length mirror and drop a pretend plumb line straight down from the top of your head to the bottom of your feet. Does it bisect you at the shoulder, the hip, the knee and the ankle bone? It should. Still not convinced? Try this test: stand normally and measure your waist. Now pull up your rib cage and measure again. Slimmer? Does it seem like magic? It's more like muscles. And muscles must be maintained to make sure you're always standing and moving prettily.

Try to make yourself think about your posture at odd moments throughout the day – play games, as it were. Pretend

Sit against wall with legs crossed, arms against wall, bent upward in right angles, all vertebrae touching wall. Slide arms up until straight above your head. Do 10 times.

Lie on the floor with arms over head, knees bent, feet flat on floor. Pull in abdomen so small of back presses against floor; hold, then relax. Do 10 times.

Lie on floor with knees bent, feet flat, arms bent at elbows. Pull in abdomen while you straighten legs and arms. Count to 10, then relax. Do 10 times.

you're a puppet on strings being pulled up, up, up. Try to touch an imaginary ceiling with the top of your head. Make believe your tummy and back are book-ends and squeeze them tightly together. Think of your body as a set of child's building bricks – stack them straight or they'll fall down.

Think about being a jack-in-the-box. Place your hands opposite each other at the back and front of your waist. Tuck down your tail, lift your stomach up and in and you'll find that your hands are no longer parallel. Applaud, as if at the theatre: clap your hands in front, above the head and behind you. Then demand an encore – just think what it's doing for those sagging shoulders – but this time with the hands back to back.

With more time to spare, do a few specific posture exercises. The three shown above are all designed to strengthen back muscles and straighten slumped shoulders and swaybacks (the two most common posture faults). Whether you choose to do one or all three, the secret is daily repetition. Work slowly and rhythmically, stretching until you feel a 'pull'.

Remember that every effort you make to improve your posture and give your movements grace, every 10 minutes you spend exercising for a trim lithe body will bring dividends – in the way your clothes fit and move, in the way you feel about yourself, in the way others see you.

General Fitness

Literally everyone – fat, thin or just right – needs exercise. Not just the muscles you use to climb stairs, load the washing-machine, do the shopping, but all the muscles need their share of activity to stay firm, strong and flexible. Even if you are an active sports fan, only a few sports – swimming, volleyball or fencing – give you muscle tone all over. Ballet and modern dance also do a good job. But if you don't go in for one of these every week of the year, the best guarantee of a complete work-out is daily exercise at home. All the authorities on the subject agree that a 10-minute daily routine is more effective than a sporadic hour-long dose when the mood moves you – though even that is better than nothing. Choose exercises you enjoy. The range is so wide you can assemble a group of exercises that perfectly suit your figure and temperament needs – fast, slow, more vigorous or less.

However unfit you are, the great joy is that even after long under-use or disuse, the muscles will still increase in girth and power if they're exercised properly again. The most important thing is to build up gradually. It's a mistake – and may even be dangerous – to go from complete inactivity to strenuous exercise all at once.

Attitudes to exercise: Choose a time and a place convenient for you. There's no ideal time of the day to exercise, although last thing at night, directly after meals and directly after getting up should be avoided.

Choose a private place unless you're making this a group project. There's something to be said for exercising in the company of a few friends, but any time the others fail to appear you might be tempted to skip the routine. Group exercising works best for weekly work-outs.

The ideal 'gym' is a well-ventilated, heated room – your bedroom is probably the best location. Rearrange furniture if necessary; the area you need for freedom of movement is ideally your height circumference. A full-length mirror enables you to check that your shoulders and face do not tense up. A cool or warm shower beforehand helps to loosen you up. *Never* exercise after a hot bath: this can not only cause an increase in blood pressure but really relaxed muscles can become strained through overdoing things. If you feel any stiffness the day after your first attempt at exercise, add a handful of relaxing bath salts to your bath water and steep in it for a while. Exercise in clothing which does not restrict you at all. The ideal flooring is an exercise mat, rug or folded blanket, which helps prevent bruising and skin irritations.

Make an exercise mat: If your exercise area does not have a rug, make an exercise mat in a colour keyed to your leotard. You'll need a pair of beach towels, a length of thin foam rubber 2.5 cm (1 inch) smaller than the towel all round (to allow for the seams) and 3 giant stud fasteners. Sew the towels together on 3 sides to enclose the foam rubber and use the stud fasteners to close the open end.

Eating Habits

A good well-balanced diet is a basic essential for top-to-toe health and the best way to achieve it is to keep to a regular meal pattern. Three meals a day – breakfast, one main meal and one light meal – should be sufficient to provide a healthy balanced diet. How can you be sure that you are getting all the vitamins and minerals that you need? Most easily by eating a wide variety of foods. There is nothing so potentially damaging both physically and mentally than a rigid and unbalanced diet adhered to for more than a few days.

Foods can be allocated to different groups based on the nutrients they contain. Two average portions of food from each of the following groups every day should provide you with enough of all these nutrients.

> Group 1: Meat, poultry, fish, eggs
> Group 2: Milk, cheese, yogurt
> Group 3: Fruit and vegetables
> Group 4: Bread, pasta, cereals
> Group 5: Butter, margarine, oils

Vegetarians, particularly those who do not eat food in groups 1 or 2, should include a wide variety of vegetable protein foods instead: pulses – lentils, kidney beans, haricot beans, chick peas, etc – nuts and cereals are particularly good sources. They also contain useful vitamins and minerals.

Of course, every person's needs are slightly different, especially as far as calorie intake is concerned. It is also important to realize that most foods in groups 1 and 2 are sources of fats (Group 5) too – weight-watchers take note!

If you find dieting difficult, make just one or two diet changes. Have a fruit breakfast, use a sweetener instead of sugar, have one starch-free meal a day. Season foods with spices or herbs or tart fruit juices – all add variety. Don't overlook psychological aids either. Eat slowly, chew well and eat from a smaller plate. Take the edge off your hunger before a meal with a snack of bouillon, a heart of lettuce or a spoonful of yogurt. When tempted to eat between meals, sip a glass of iced water or eat a bit of cheese with a stick of celery or a tomato.

Excess weight often means faulty elimination. Check this. One cause is a high starch, low vitamin diet. As far as possible, avoid white bread, white sugar, white polished rice, cakes, sweets, buns and biscuits and have plenty of protein foods, lightly cooked vegetables, salads and fruit.

Another cause is not enough bulk or roughage in the diet. One of the best ways of overcoming this is to take a bran cereal for breakfast. Make sure that you are also taking enough Vitamin B foods. A daily dose of wheatgerm will often cure

constipation. Make sure that you drink enough water; if you are not regular, try drinking 5 glasses a day between meals.

Although it is true that many people gain a few pounds in weight during the winter, there is no need to regard an increase as inevitable. It's important to keep up the intake of Vitamins A and D during the winter: fresh fruits and vegetables are just as important to winter good looks as they are in summer.

Weight is closely related to metabolism, which governs how fast you burn up the calories you take in when you eat. The metabolic rate is faster in some people than in others, which may partly explain why every chocolate you swallow seems to show while your best friend can live on pasta without seeming to gain an ounce! She may also be much more active and/or tense than you are. Slow metabolism is a favourite excuse for excess pounds, but in fact most people have normal metabolism. The rate does change at different ages however. Growth helps raise the body's basic energy expenditure. Adults use less energy per pound than teenagers.

Calories are energy units and it is not until we are either over-weight or under-weight that we need to worry about them. Cutting down on calories does not mean starving but choosing low calorie foods. For example, a lean lamb cutlet provides 100 calories, so does a chocolate cream!

It takes time to break old eating habits, to plan healthy meals or appetizing low-calorie ones. Ideally, let all the family co-operate with you in planning meals two or three days ahead. If you're one of a large family this helps with the shopping and keeps you organized. There is little chance of error if you add up the calories before instead of after you eat. A slim, firm figure is not the only bonus. Add to that clear skin, bright shiny eyes and swinging vibrant hair.

Stress

Stress means different things to different people. Most of us would bracket it with some sort of distress: the distress of sitting up night after night studying, fearful of doing badly in an exam; the distress of running a home on a tight budget, having to shop around, getting tired; the distress of being burdened with elderly parents, having to cope with their problems as well as your own. Stress becomes bottled up inside you. Things like traffic jams, long delays in queues, waiting endlessly for the phone to ring all contribute to a feeling of being wound up internally. For most of us these are isolated examples, but when an anxiety endures and develops into prolonged stress then the body simply wears down.

Signs of stress you can quickly recognize include poor sleep, over-eating or drinking, hunched tense posture and repetitive mannerisms like teeth-clenching, nail-biting or pencil-tapping.

Preventatives: Stress can be alleviated by mental discipline, conscious relaxation and the right kind of food. Let's start with those often vague feelings of worry, rather than actual problems, which often make us tense.

Before going to bed, aim to empty your mind of worries. Take paper and pencil and drag them out into the open, writing down every mild nag in your mind. Having written them down, study them carefully. Can you do anything about this one, for example? No? Then take your pencil and strike it out. The very act of putting your pencil through it will get it off your mind. This worry now? You can do something about that! Well, write down just what you can do and resolve to do it on such and such a date. Do this every night, clearing your mind of worried feelings and watch your stress symptoms disappear.

Watch for points of tension and strain. These are usually the shoulders, hands, feet and face. Check the position of the shoulders frequently. We tend to hold them tensely, sometimes pulling them up almost to the ears. Relax them. Do a few shoulder circling movements. Flap the hands loosely from the wrists to relax them. Make sure that when you are sitting, your legs are not wound round each other or the ankles round the legs of the chair. To relieve neck and shoulder tension, try these spot-relaxers:

1. Shrug your shoulders to your ears – one shoulder at a time – and circle forward 6 times, now backwards 6 times.

2. Relax shoulders and gently roll the head to a full circle, first round to the right, then to the left. Repeat 3 times each side.

3. Not an exercise, but sleeping with a Chinese pillow will help alleviate any unusual sleeping angles which contribute to tension in the neck.

Cures: A course of body massage is a very good antidote to stress and the gentle stroking and manipulating of the spine is ideal for relaxing a tense body. A warm bath, containing some pleasant-smelling herb or perfumed bath essence, is another way of relaxing. So is scalp massage – you can massage your own scalp quite easily, working with gentle circular movements from hairline to crown. Hair-brushing with rubber-based bristles is a very relaxing bedtime exercise. A few minutes face massage every night at bedtime is helpful to relax tense muscles, particularly from the area above the nose up to the hairline of the forehead, along the eyebrows, the temples and the area about the eyes.

Increasing your intake of thiamin (Vitamin B_1) may help. Thiamin is found in whole grains, sunflower seeds, chicken, fish roe, sardines, cod, lean beef, liver, pork and kidney.

Relaxing beverages (and sleep inducing!) include the following: peppermint tea, sweetened with a teaspoonful of honey; a glass of hot milk with 9 drops of oil of cloves added; a cup of lime tisane; orange flower water (an old French cure for sleeplessness) – 1 tablespoon orange flower water in a wine glassful of warm water with a lump of sugar; 1 tablespoon honey taken in hot water, with or without the juice of half a lemon.

SHAPING UP

SHAPING UP

Body types: First of all get to know your body type. Don't judge yourself on model girl proportions. Your body type holds the key to your scope for improvement. Your figure fits into one of three categories, which can't be altered, but you can certainly aim for better proportions. It is possible to alter the shape of any part of the body. The only unalterables are the length of your bones. But even the spine can be stretched a little, especially if there is bad posture, which could result in 0.5-1 cm (¼-½ inch) difference in height.

Now for the three body types. If you are an *ectomorph*, small framed with narrow shoulders and often even narrower hips, you should aim to be neat-waisted with little obvious muscle or fat. A *mesomorph* with a medium to large frame, ranging from quite square and angular to comfortably rounded, often with broad shoulders, should be mostly muscle and bone with not much obvious fat and a slim line right through waist and hips. An *endomorph*, heavily built but not necessarily large framed, is sturdy through rib cage, waist and hips and usually quite well covered, but ideally has trim muscles and no excess fat.

Capacity for exercise: Your preference and aptitude for certain types of exercise and sport is often dictated by your figure type. Ideally, settle for those you can perform with enjoyment and a sense of achievement. Don't struggle fruitlessly with an exercise form with which you are not physically compatible.

Ectomorphs usually display qualities of endurance and agility and have good body support, all of which links them with such diverse sports as cross-country running and volleyball. In between, of course, that leaves anything from running, jogging, hiking, skiing, badminton and tennis.

Mesomorphs, with a traditionally muscular frame and scope for developing strength, endurance, power and agility, can be good at just about anything they try, be it running or weight training.

Endomorphs don't rate top marks for strength, agility, endurance, power or body strength. Most true endomorphs will happily admit to being less sporty than many of their acquaintance, having long since discovered that they are better working at their own pace. Favourite activities include those which don't necessarily embrace a competitive element. Things like swimming, cycling, archery and bowling are ideal.

Weight: What Should You Weigh

It is a good idea to monitor your weight level. Ideally, weigh yourself once a week, on the same scales, at the same time of day, wearing the same clothes – or nothing at all. If you are fully dressed, including shoes, allow 2.75 kg (6 lb) for the weight of winter clothes, 1.75 kg (4 lb) for summer clothes.

When you are trying to lose weight, it is a temptation to weigh yourself every day, particularly if you have your own bathroom scales – but this is a mistake. Weight does not drop off regularly but in fits and starts, and the daily check might well discourage you. As a rough guide, aim to stay within 2.25 kg (5 lb) of the normal weight for your body type/frame.

From the mid-thirties onwards, metabolism slows down and needs about 100 calories a day fewer than it did 10 years ago. While this might not sound much, an extra 100 calories a day can add up to about 4.5 kg (10 lb) a year! That's how weight creeps on. Admittedly, there are times in a woman's life when there is a tendency to put on weight: adolescence; after having a baby; or at the menopause. These phases need only be temporary.

How do you assess your type of frame or build? You don't know whether you come in the small, medium or large category? The type of frame you have conditions your weight quite considerably. To find out which section you come under, measure your wrist. If it is less than 14 cm (5½ inches) you have a small frame; 14-16 cm (5½-6½ inches) a medium frame; over 16 cm (6½ inches) a large frame. There are always exceptions to this rule, but it is a good general guide.

How do you know when you are fat? Generally, a doctor will say that you are definitely over-weight if your weight is 10-15 per cent more than that indicated for your frame and height. A variation of 5-10 per cent over or under is generally believed to have no effect upon your health.

Don't feel discouraged if your weight doesn't tumble down accommodatingly after days or even weeks on a strict diet, even though on checking your measurements you find that your inches are a little less. There is a simple reason for this: when a fat cell shrinks through lack of nourishment, it leaves a space which fills up with water – water weighs more than fat – hence no noticeable difference may be registered for quite a while on the scales, though clothes seem to fit better.

What should you weigh?
Desirable weight, without clothes, for women aged 25 plus

Height	Small frame	Medium frame	Large frame
ft. ins.	st. lb.	st. lb.	st. lb.
4 10	6 13	7 6	8 2
4 11	7 2	7 9	8 5
5 0	7 5	7 12	8 8
5 1	7 8	8 1	8 11
5 2	7 11	8 5	9 1
5 3	8 0	8 8	9 5
5 4	8 4	8 13	9 9
5 5	8 9	9 3	9 13
5 6	8 11	9 7	10 3
5 7	9 2	9 11	10 6
5 8	9 6	10 1	10 11
5 9	9 10	10 5	11 2
5 10	10 00	10 9	11 6

Measurements: Measuring up to Ideals

Once you start to lose weight, fat accumulation becomes a diminishing problem. In over-weight, fat tends to accumulate initially in the fat depots, sited in the tummy and waistline areas, the top of the thighs and the upper arms. Only in gross obesity does the body store away weight in other areas. It is impossible to say where any individual will lose fat or bulges first; for some it may be from the waistline, for others the thighs.

If you want to embark on a realignment programme, you should allow from 2 to 12 weeks depending on the amount of reshaping you want to accomplish. You should not try to lose more than 750 g (1½ lb) per week unless you are extremely overweight to begin with. Combining diet and exercise you may be able to remove as much as 2.5 cm (1 inch) a month from fleshy areas. Thus if you want to take off 4.5 kg (10 lb), 2.5 cm (1 inch) from your waist and 5 cm (2 inches) from your hips, you should allow about 10 weeks in which to accomplish your goal.

The chart below gives an indication of how long it should take to lose weight on a sensible diet. Set your own target date and work towards it. Remember it is always advisable to check with your doctor if you want to lose more than 2.75 kg (6 lb).

How long does it take to get rid of bulges?		
Your present weight	**Amount you want to lose**	**Maximum time it should take**
Between 8 st.3 lb and 8 st.13 lb	5 lb	4 weeks
	10 lb	8 weeks
Between 8 st.13 lb and 9 st.9 lb	5 lb	3 weeks
	10 lb	6 weeks
	20 lb	12 weeks
Between 9 st.9 lb and 10 st.5 lb	5 lb	2½ weeks
	10 lb	5 weeks
	20 lb	11 weeks
Between 10 st.5 lb and 11 st.11 lb	5 lb	2 weeks
	10 lb	4 weeks
	20 lb	9 weeks

The ideal scale of measurements is as follows: bust and hips should measure the same; waist should be 25 cm (10 inches) smaller than bust; thighs should be about 15 cm (6 inches) less than waist; calves about 15-18 cm (6-7 inches) less than thighs; ankles about 13-15 cm (5-6 inches) less than calves; and upper arms should be double the size of wrists.

Where to measure: Here are the instructions for taking accurate readings. *Chest:* under armpits, straight around. *Upper arm:* 10 cm (4 inches) down from armpit, then around. *Bust:* straight across back and over the fullest part of the bust. *Waist:* smallest part. *Abdomen:* across the navel, around back, below waist. *Upper hips:* halfway between abdomen and lower hips. *Lower hips:* around the largest part of buttocks. *Top thigh:* up under leg as high as possible, and straight around. *Mid-thigh:* halfway between top thigh measure and knee. *Knee:* around the middle. *Calf:* around the largest part. *Ankle:* around the smallest part, just above ankle bone. Take all measurements with muscles relaxed, and always measure the same limb – right and left limb measurement may be different.

Ideally, measure yourself before you embark on a diet and exercise régime then wait 10 days before taking your measurements again; then another 10 days, and so on.

Always been on the plump side as far back as you can remember? Then double check to see if you are carrying abnormal amounts of body fat. One way of finding out is to lie flat on your back with a ruler on your front. If your weight is normal, the ruler can touch both your ribs and your pelvis. If one end sticks up in the air, it means that something, like fat, is pushing it out.

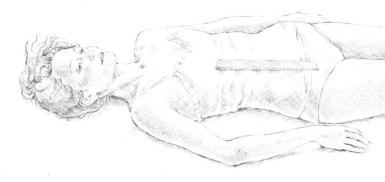

Alternatively, take a deep pinch of skin on your side, just over the lower ribs. If the distance between thumb and index finger is greater than 2.5 cm (1 inch), you are probably too fat. If it is less than 1 cm (½ inch), you are probably too thin. Perfect proportions are, of course, the exception rather than the rule. They should be used as a guide rather than a goal. The best practice is to subtract your ideal measurements from your actual measurements to determine the degree of difference, then strive to cut that difference in half. Thus, if your actual measurements are bust 87 cm (34 inches), waist 66 cm

110

(26 inches), hips 97 cm (38 inches), and your ideal measurements are bust 87 cm (34 inches), waist 61 cm (24 inches), hips 87 cm (34 inches), your goal would be bust 87 cm (34 inches), waist 64 cm (25 inches) and hips 92 cm (36 inches).

Few of us possess ideal proportions – most of us have at least one main figure fault in need of correction. While diet and exercise are often the answer, they cannot alter bone structure. However, the right choice of clothes for your figure type can give imperfect proportions the illusion of perfection.

Ectomorphs, those with the so-called average figure, are fairly evenly proportioned all over; any silhouette is good on them whether waistlines go up, down or stay put.

The broad-shouldered mesomorph needs emphasis below the waist to balance her light-bulb silhouette. That means keeping major pattern and colour accents below the waist, with everything above under-stated and non-clingy. This figure type looks great in trousers of all lengths.

The sturdy, usually well-rounded endomorph looks best in classic trim shapes with soft, rather than very tailored outlines. Medium length jackets are good for this figure and it pays to keep major accents small in scale most of the time.

EXERCISE

EXERCISE

Greater physical fitness is within the grasp of anyone willing to exercise regularly. And it can be fun. So what do we really know about exercise?

It isn't a question of jogging being good or bad, or tennis being better than badminton. What is clear is that any physical activity – any exertion at all – increases your potential for physical ability. And that's what exercise is all about. It doesn't matter whether you can run faster, swim harder or lift heavier weights than the next man, woman or child. It does matter, at any age, if you find it an effort to run the length of the bus stop, to climb the stairs to the top deck, or even to ease yourself out of a sitting position in the evening.

Once you've managed to get over the hurdle of thinking that exercise is a burdensome chore, are beginning to enjoy it and count the blessings of your increased fitness, you're ready to go on to a specific exercise routine. The ideal programme should progress and exercise the body in every way, which means that the programme should include exercises of three different types: for suppleness (mobility); for strength; for stamina (heart and lung exercises).

Mobility exercises persuade the major joints and muscles to move through their complete range of movement. Eventually, as you progress, you will find that you can turn, stretch, twist in every direction with greater freedom and grace.

Male or female, old or young, we all need a certain amount of muscle strength so that we can lift, pull, push or carry heavy objects when necessary. Strength is developed by exercising the limbs and trunk against resistance.

Stamina is dependent on the efficiency of the heart and lungs. To exercise these organs we have to increase the oxygen requirements of the body and this is most easily done by exercising the legs, arms and trunk. This is where running, jogging and ball games come in – and this is where so many people worry about the possibility of heart attack. It's generally advised that no one over fifty, overweight or with a history of heart disease should start any kind of exercise programme without consulting a doctor.

The exercises in this chapter cover the full spectrum. Some are in two stages: beginners and advanced. That way you can learn an exercise efficiently and then go on to develop its full potential. Do not be in a hurry to progress – wait until you can do the full number of repetitions comfortably at the first level.

General Exercise Plan

TOE TOUCH FOR BEGINNERS:
Stand erect, feet slightly apart,
hands over head. Bend forward
from waist to touch toes with
fingertips. Keep knees straight

even if you can't reach toes at
first. Return to standing
position before repeating. Begin
with 20, gradually speed up
to 40.

TOE TOUCH, ADVANCED PLAN:
Stand erect, feet about 40 cm
(16 inches) apart, toes pointed
out, arms extended straight out
from shoulders. Keep arms
straight and bend from waist to

touch left foot with right hand.
Do not bend knees. Return to
starting position, then repeat on
other side, touching right foot
with left hand. Begin with 15,
gradually increase to 25.

BENDS FOR BEGINNERS: Stand erect, feet about 30 cm (12 inches) apart, hands clasped together over head. Bend from the waist to right side, keeping back straight and arms extended. Return to starting position, then bend to other side. Continue, alternating sides. Begin with 10 on each side, increase to 20.

ADVANCED BENDS: Stand erect, feet 30 cm (12 inches) apart, arms extended. Bend right arm over head, dropping left arm to side. Keep back straight and bend from waist. Slide left arm down leg as far as possible. Return to start and repeat on other side. Begin with 10 each side, increase to 20.

KNEES BEND: Stand erect, feet together, arms forward, Rise upon toes, then slowly bend knees. Keep back straight and arms extended. Return to start at same speed. Begin with 10, work up to 20.

117

ARM SWING FOR BEGINNERS:
Stand erect, feet together, arms
extended in front with hands
about waist level. Swing arms
around and as far back as they
will go, then swing forward to
starting position. Begin with
25, gradually increasing speed
to 50.

ARM SWING, ADVANCED PLAN:
Stand erect, feet together, arms
extended straight forward at
shoulder level. Keeping arms
straight, swing them around
and as far back as they will go.
Keep arms at shoulder level and
swing back to starting position.
Begin with 40, increase to 60.

HIP ROLL: Lie flat on back, legs
together, arms extended from
shoulders, palms down. Keep
legs together and tuck up close to
chest. Keeping knees together
and shoulders on floor, roll over

to left side until left leg is flat on
floor. Keeping legs tucked up,
roll back until right leg is flat on
floor. Begin by touching each
leg to the floor 10 times, work
up to 25 each side.

SIT-UPS FOR BEGINNERS: *Lie on back, legs straight and together, arms extended over head. Keep legs in position, back as straight as possible and move to a sitting position. Bend from the waist to touch toes with hands. Return at same speed to starting position. Begin with 10, work up to 25.*

SIT-UPS, ADVANCED PLAN: *Lie on back, legs straight and together, hands clasped behind head. Keep legs in position, back as straight as possible and move to sitting position. Bend forward with head down. Return at same speed to starting position. Hold abdomen in throughout. Start with 20, work up to 35.*

119

LEG SWING: Stand erect, feet together, left hand on wall for support, right hand at side. Keeping back and legs straight, swing right leg up, then down and back. Point toes and reach as high as possible. Swing 10 times. Reverse position and repeat with left leg. Work up to 20.

LEG KICK: Lie on side, legs straight, head on extended lower arm. Use other arm for balance. Keeping legs straight, raise upper leg until perpendicular to floor, then lower to start position. Begin with 10 each leg, work up to 20.

RUNNING ON SPOT: Stand erect, feet together, hands on hips. Run on spot, raising knees higher and increasing speed as you go.

PUSH-UPS FOR BEGINNERS:
Lie face down, legs together,
forearms along floor with
elbows directly under shoulders.
Raise body from the floor by
straightening back. Balance on
toes and elbows. Lower body
back to floor and repeat without
resting in between. Begin with
5, gradually work up to 15.

PUSH-UPS, ADVANCED PLAN:
Lie face down, legs straight and
together, hands flat and
pointing forward directly under
shoulders. Push body up from
hands and toes until arms are
fully extended. Keep body and
legs in straight line and lower by
bending elbows. Touch chest to
floor and repeat without resting.
Begin with 3, gradually work
up to 10.

121

Eliminating Figure Faults

The exercises on the following pages are designed to correct common figure problems in 10 areas of the body:

Bustline: Exercise will strengthen the muscles which support your bust. It won't add much to the size, but it will firm and uplift, giving you a prettier contour. The same exercises will also make your bust seem larger by correcting shoulder slump.

Upper arms: The muscles in the upper arms are among the most neglected in a woman's body. Exercise is essential to prevent and correct flabbiness.

Midriff: Exercise combined with good posture will quickly flatten and firm this area while increasing its flexibility.

Waistline: Exercise works wonders in whittling away excess inches in this crucial area.

Abdomen: The key to a flat tummy is strong abdominal muscles, which are readily attained with persistent exercise.

Bottom: Exercise reduces the fat in this area and strengthens the muscles which control firmness.

Hips: There are many exercises which will reduce and firm the flesh in this area, even without loss of weight.

Thighs: Persistent exercise will turn flabbiness into firmness while slowly whittling off an inch or two.

Calves: The same exercises that slim down heavy calves will also add pretty curves to thin ones.

Ankles: Exercise cannot perform miracles but it can trim as much as 2-3 cm (1 inch) off your ankles. It also tones and strengthens the muscles.

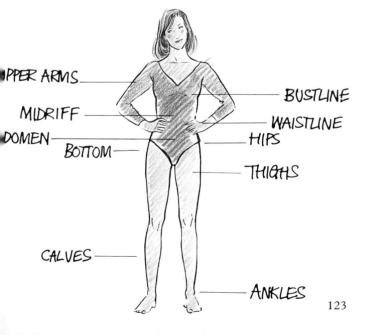

UPPER ARMS — BUSTLINE
MIDRIFF — WAISTLINE
ABDOMEN — BOTTOM — HIPS
THIGHS
CALVES
ANKLES

Bust

Stand erect, feet together, arms at sides. Hold weights in each hand (such as full soft drink bottles or polythene containers of salt or vinegar). Lift hands over head, then swing back down and around to form a complete circle with each hand. Begin with 10 circles, work up to 20.

Stand erect, elbows bent, finger-tips touching in front of chin. Keep arms at shoulder level and pull elbows back as far as they go. Return to start and repeat. Begin with 5, work up to 15.

124

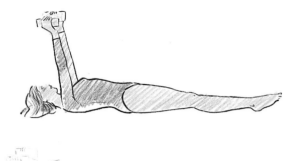

Upper Arms

Lie down, legs together, arms at sides, hands holding weights (such as full soft drink bottles or polythene containers full of salt). Keeping arms straight, lift weights until arms are fully extended above your head. Slowly lower hands to shoulders, then return to starting position. Begin with 10, work up to 20.

Stand erect, feet apart, hands clasped behind back. Keeping back and arms straight, lift hands as high as you can. Return to start, relax and repeat. Begin with 5, work up to 10.

Midriff
Sit on the floor with legs straight, feet as far apart as possible. Lift left arm over your head and bend to touch right foot with right hand. Return to starting position, then bend to the left. Begin with 5 bends in each direction, work up to 10.

Lie down with knees pulled up to chest, arms at sides. Lift legs straight up, then back over head, using hands to support hips. Return to starting position and repeat. Begin with 5, work up to 10.

Waistline
Stand erect, feet together, arms extended over head. Keep legs straight and bend from waist to touch toes. Return to starting position, then bend back from the waist. Begin with 10, work up to 25.

Sit on floor with legs straight and feet as far apart as possible, hands clasped behind head. Twist to touch right knee with left elbow. Return to starting position, then touch left knee with right elbow. Begin with 5 twists each side, work up to 10.

127

Abdomen

Lie on floor, legs together, hands clasped under head. Keeping toes pointed and knees straight, lift legs very slowly until pointing to the ceiling. Lower them back into position equally slowly, contracting abdominal muscles as you do so. Begin with 3, work up to 10.

Lie face down, legs together, arms straight at sides. Keeping your legs straight and together, and your toes pointed, lift shoulders and feet from the floor simultaneously so that your body forms an arc. Begin with 5, gradually work up to 10.

128

Bottom

Lie on floor, arms outstretched from shoulders, palms down. Bend knees, pulling feet as close to buttocks as possible. Contract bottom muscles and press hips upwards into thighs, raising lower back off the floor. Hold for a count of 5, then drop quickly back to starting position. Begin with 5, work up to 15.

Sit Indian-fashion, with soles of feet together, hands on ankles. Keep your back straight and rock from side to side. Begin with 10 rocks to each side, work up to 20.

Hips

Lie down, legs straight, arms at sides, palms down. Point toes and lift legs as high as possible, then slowly move them up and

down alternately in a bicycle motion. Support hips with your hands if necessary. Begin with 15 complete circles, work up to 25.

Lie down, knees bent, feet on floor, arms extended from the shoulders, palms downwards. Keeping shoulders flat on the floor and knees together,

roll legs rapidly to slap floor on the right, reversing to slap floor on the left. Begin with 10 rolls to each side, work up to 20.

Thighs

Lie on floor, legs straight, arms at sides, palms down. Lift both legs about 25 cm (10 inches) from the floor, then swing them apart as wide as possible. Swing together, then apart 3 more times before returning to starting position. Begin with 5, work up to 10.

Sit with knees bent, hands and feet resting on floor, as close to your body as possible. Lift up your hips, moving them forward until your knees touch the floor. Return to starting position. Begin with 5, gradually working up to 10.

131

Calves

Stand erect, feet 40 cm (16 inches) apart, right foot turned to side, hands on hips. Lower body to floor, bending right knee, keeping left leg straight. Bob up and down several times, then return to starting position. Repeat on left side. Begin with 5 on each side, work up to 10.

Stand erect, feet together, hands on hips. Lift right knee until thigh is perpendicular to body. With toes pointed, rotate lower leg from knee to draw a circle.

Make 5 circles in each direction before returning to starting position. Repeat with left leg. Begin with 3 for each leg, work up to 8.

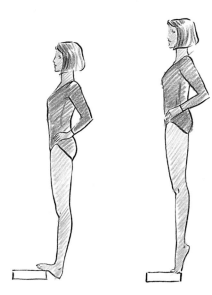

Ankles

Stand erect, hands on hips, feet together, toes resting on a large book, heels on floor. Lift heels from the floor until you are balancing on toes on edge of book. Begin with 5, work up to 10.

Lie down, legs straight, arms at sides, palms down. Lift right leg about 25 cm (10 inches) from floor and rotate foot from ankle, making a big circle with your big toe. Make 5 circles in each direction, then repeat with left foot. Do 3 or 4 times each side.

Daily Dozen

You don't need access to a gym, elaborate equipment or a figure-hugging leotard in order to exercise. There are many excellent exercises you can do at any stage in the day while sitting at your desk or working around the house. Some of these exercises are explained on the following pages. Develop the 'exercise break' habit, for a minute here and a minute there soon add up to a slimmer, trimmer figure.

For instance, aim to bend from your waist or knees instead of stooping, for proper movement is essential to good posture. Deep breathing is excellent for slimming abdomen, increasing flexibility and eliminating fatigue. When you're sitting, simple contraction of abdomen and buttocks is one of the best possible exercises for flattening and firming both areas. One way of keeping the body supple and flexible is to stretch when reaching for objects which are almost – but not quite – out of reach.

At home: When you wash dishes or peel vegetables, don't hunch over the sink: stand upright in an easy relaxed position.

When you brush your teeth, pull in your tummy muscles as if trying to touch them to your spine. Breathing quite normally, hold them there until you have finished brushing.

As you go through a door, stretch up your right hand as if trying to reach the doorway top. Then try to touch it with your left hand. This stretches and slims waist and diaphragm.

Give some thought to heel height. The lower the heel, the better legs are exercised naturally, but as each heel height exercises muscles others don't – vary your shoes.

When sitting, tighten the abdominal and buttock muscles. Hold as long as you can, relax, then repeat.

ABOVE: *When making beds, bend from the waist and stretch your body across the width of the bed. Keep your back as straight as possible when performing all such household chores.*

LEFT: *Stand in front of an open window and breathe deeply, rising up on your toes and flinging your arms wide. Exhale, relax and repeat 5 times.*

RIGHT: *Never use a footstool or ladder unless absolutely necessary. Stretch your body from head to toe when reaching for out-of-the-way objects.*

135

Every time you bend, perform an exercise. Standing up and bending from the waist exercises muscles in the backs of the legs and slims the waistline. Sitting down and bending over to the floor at the side is excellent for slimming waist and midriff. Another way to pick up something from the floor is to stand near the object and kneel on one knee before picking it up. As you rise, use your thigh muscles not the muscles of your back. This helps to keep slender thighs and prevent back strain.

Don't forget about exercising in bed or in the bath. In the bath, for instance, you can slim waist and diaphragm by keeping the legs straight and touching left foot with right hand and right foot with left hand. When drying yourself, take the towel and hold it near the centre with both hands. With bent elbows, swing arms to right at shoulder level and wring towel hard. Swing to left and wring again. Good for firming the bust.

Worried about a double chin? Before you get up in the morning, lie on your back, head extended over the edge of your bed. Let your head drop backwards, then raise it up and forwards onto your chest.

For a firm bosom, lie on top of your bed with the upper part of your body supported and make strong swimming motions with your arms. Or clench your fists and tuck them into your armpits, then make circles with your elbows as if trying to fly.

Pick up non-heavy objects from the floor by bending from the waist, keeping your legs straight; this exercises muscles in backs of legs and slims the waistline.

An alternative way of picking up objects from the floor is to sit on a straight chair or stool and bend over to the side, keeping your back straight; excellent for slimming waist and midriff.

At the office: An exercise to strengthen upper arm and chest muscles is shown above: Prop your right elbow on the desk and balance a heavy book on your fingertips. Lift the book up until the arm is fully extended above your head. Lower and repeat 5 times, then switch the book to the other hand.

Here are 2 good leg exercises. Sit on a desk or table and bend the right foot upwards from the ankle as far as it will go, then downwards. Repeat this with the left foot and finally with both feet together. Alternatively, place a telephone book at your feet. Slipping off your shoes, put one foot on the book, the foot turned slightly inwards, toes hanging over the edge. Then stretch toes down towards the floor but keep heel flat on book.

Do a few facial exercises. To help alleviate vertical frown lines, pull your eyebrows way down over your eyes. In other words, frown so hard it feels as though you were trying to get your eyebrows to meet each other end on. Then lift your eyebrows as high – and open your eyes as wide – as you can.

To help tone upper eyelids, open your mouth slightly, raise your eyebrows and close your eyes. As you raise your eyebrows up, stretch forward with your eyelids. Feel as if you're trying to get the greatest possible distance between your eyebrows and lashes. Hold for a count of 10. Very slowly and consciously, relax the eyelids, returning eyebrows to normal position.

137

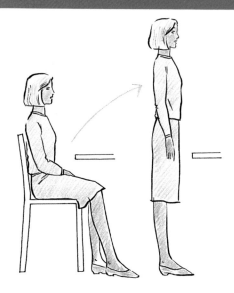

Sit erectly with your back straight, feet flat on the floor, right foot slightly forward, hands in your lap. Rise to a standing position using only your leg muscles. Lower yourself slowly back into position. Repeat when you have occasion to get in or out of your seat. This movement strengthens leg muscles and helps slim calves and thighs.

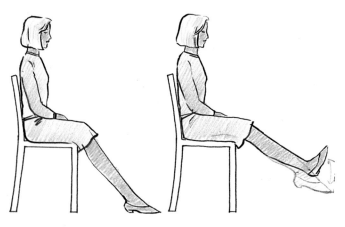

Stretch your legs out in front of you with toes pointed. Lift both feet up about 30 cm (12 inches) from the floor. Keeping knees together and legs straight, move your feet rapidly up and down scissor-fashion. This stimulates leg circulation and strengthens muscles.

Place both hands on your desk, palms down, fingers together, elbows bent. Press down in an effort to lift your body slightly from the chair. Hold pressure for a few seconds, then relax. This tones and strengthens muscles of the shoulders and upper arms.

Rotate your head in a wide circle from the base of your neck. Begin with 2 circles, work up to 5. This tones the neck muscles and helps to keep chin and neck firm.

Cross your legs, right over left, with toes pointed. Rotate your right foot from the ankle as if you were drawing a wide circle with your big toe. Make

5 circles in each direction, then repeat with your left foot. An excellent exercise for strengthening and slimming the ankles.

139

Good Sports

Outdoor activities like tennis, skiing and swimming are excellent forms of exercise. Indoor movements which stimulate the muscles used in these sports are good fun and help achieve better results when you come to do the real thing. Apart from anything else, they build up confidence and an awareness of the joints and muscles that are most in play.

The tennis routine is designed to keep joints mobile, muscles flexible, and eye and foot control co-ordinated. A pre-ski programme should ideally start several months before you set off for the slopes. Running, jogging, jumping and skipping, climbing stairs, learning to balance on one leg will all help prepare the body for the rigours of the ski scene. Although there is no need to be fit to enjoy a swim, power and efficiency in the water can be greatly enhanced by exercising on dry land.

So when the weather goes against you, don't despair: keep in trim with an indoor routine. And when the sun shines or the snow is right and you're going to do the real thing, these basic exercises are particularly effective as warm-ups.

Tennis routine

Stand erect, feet 15 cm (6 inches) apart, hands clasped together behind back. Keeping back and arms straight, lift hands as high as you can. Return to start. Begin with 5, work up to 10.

Stand erect, feet about 30 cm (12 inches) apart, hands clasped together over head. Bend from the waist to right side, keeping back straight and arms extended. Return to starting position, then bend to other side. 10 on each side.

Sit on floor, hugging head to knees, arms clasped round legs, feet together. Holding position, rock backwards, until back touches floor. Rock back and forth gently 8 to 10 times.

Skiing routine
Stand erect, arms by your sides. Keeping feet flat on floor, raise arms as high as you can for a count of 5. Lower them slowly.

Stand with arms raised above head and, moving from waist up, swing arms as far to the left as possible, then to the right. Do 4 times.

Stand erect with your arms raised at the sides to shoulder level. Swing arms back as far as you can. Then swing them forward. Repeat up to 6 times.

Stand erect, feet together, arms raised behind you, palms up. Bend knees as far as you can; keep upper body straight. Slowly straighten up. Repeat 4 times.

Stand erect, feet together. Keeping body straight and feet flat on floor, bend knees, twisting them to the left. Straighten and twist to the right. Repeat 4 times.

Stand erect, feet together, right heel against a sturdy chair leg. Bend knees and swing to right, aiming to clasp chair leg with left hand. Do 4 times each side.

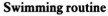

Swimming routine
Lie face down on the bed, feet together, hips supported by bed, upper body projecting over side. Keep legs, body and head straight. Gradually lower body until elbows and forehead touch floor. Slowly straighten arms and raise head and body to starting position. Repeat 3 to 4 times.

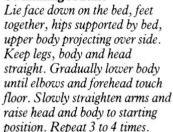

Lie flat on your back and, keeping legs together, bring your knees up over your chest – as far as you can. Clasp hands over ankles and try to touch knees with forehead. Slowly straighten legs to lie flat again. Repeat 2 to 3 times.

Sit on the floor with knees bent and feet tucked under buttocks. With hands on floor behind you, lean back, raising your knees to stretch ankles. Repeat 5 times.

Stand with your arms raised to shoulder height in front of you, palms together. Keeping arms at shoulder level, pull them back hard to sides. Repeat 5 times.

143

Pregnancy

Even if the idea of exercising is your pet aversion, overcome it during pregnancy: your figure and general health will benefit enormously and with muscles in good strong condition, no special maternity underpinnings should be necessary. Most doctors agree that plenty of fresh air and exercise are important for good general health and to keep muscles in fine tone. But violent exercise is best avoided, especially during the last few months, and don't, at any time, go lugging at – or trying to lift – heavy objects.

The healthy way is to carry on with normal daily work but to do as much of it as possible sitting down – and miss no opportunity of putting your feet up. Aim to do one or two foot exercises every day, if only to encourage you to sit down. For instance, with your heels resting on the floor, bend your feet upward from the ankle. Bend your feet down again. Repeat often during the day. Or, with your heels resting on the floor, curl up your toes tightly, straighten out and repeat.

It is extremely good for women in the later stages of pregnancy to spend some time each day relaxing with their feet up. Raising the feet higher than the hips relieves pressure on the pelvic veins, aids circulation in the legs and helps to prevent varicose veins and swollen ankles. Pain in the tail bone

is quite common during pregnancy, depending on the extra weight involved. Try placing a cushion under your thighs for relief when sitting.

Eating correctly ensures that you do not put on unnecessary weight, and correct posture and gentle controlled exercise ensure that after the baby is born the body returns quickly and easily to its former shape.

Once your doctor or midwife has given you the go-head to start working your way back to your normal weight and shape, limber up every day – on waking – by stretching every part of your anatomy.

Still lying in bed, on a hard mattress if possible, bend your right knee up to your chin, holding it there with your hands. Slowly lift head, neck and shoulders up as you pull your knee closer and closer. Hold for a count of 5, then relax as you lower your head back down. Repeat with the left leg.

Lie on your back with your legs out straight. Keeping your heels on the bed, make small circling movements with your feet, first inwards, then outwards.

Lie on your back with both knees raised and your feet flat on the bed. Pull in the muscles of your abdomen and slowly roll your knees over to the right, then back up again. Repeat, rolling to the left.

145

Before: Good posture is vital during pregnancy; the hollow backward-leaning stance is one of the most common causes of backache in pregnant women. Also, it is important to learn to contract the pelvic floor muscles if their elasticity is to be retained after the birth. General exercises are also valuable.

Lie on your back with knees bent and feet flat. Breathing normally, tighten your buttock muscles by squeezing the two sides of your bottom together

and, at the same time, pull in your abdominal muscles to feel the hollow of your back press against floor. Hold for 5 seconds, then relax. Do 5 times slowly.

Kneel on all fours with knees directly below your hips and your hands directly below your shoulders. Slowly arch your

back and draw in your pelvis, tucking in your seat. Hold this arched position for 5 seconds, then relax. Repeat 6 to 8 times.

Lie on your back with your knees bent and your feet flat. Straighten your left knee to

extend your leg along the floor. Repeat with right leg. Repeat 5 to 10 times with each leg.

146

After: During pregnancy, muscles in the abdomen, pelvic region and rib cage become stretched, and often, as physical activities are restricted, other muscles of the body lose their tone. These exercises are designed to strengthen the stretched – as well as the little-used – muscles and to help get the organs in the abdominal cavity back into position. Always ask your doctor's advice about when to start exercising and which exercises you should tackle: 6 to 10 days after the birth is usually about right. Do the following exercises daily.

Lie on your back with knees bent, feet flat and hands on thighs. Pulling in your abdominal muscles and raising your head and shoulders slightly, slide your hands slowly along your thighs towards your knees. Slowly slide your hands back again and lie flat. Repeat 10 to 12 times, working up to 24.

Lie on your back with knees bent and feet flat. Place arms out to the sides with elbows straight and hands at hip level, palms up. With arms straight, reach over with your left hand to touch your right hand, raising your head to look at your hands. Repeat on other side. Repeat 5 times, working up to 24.

SLEEP AND
RELAXATION

SLEEP AND RELAXATION

How to relax, how to let yourself go – even if it is just for a few minutes every day or for a good night's sleep – is a secret well worth knowing. It really doesn't matter how busy you are at home with your household chores and children, or at work with a profession, learning to relax and being able to enjoy sound sleep are the secrets of peace of mind and happiness.

Sleep

A minimum of 8 hours sleep each night is a necessity for beauty, and an extra bonus of sleep each night will often improve the looks as much as a holiday. When eyes are tired, the complexion drab and the spirits low, the cure can often be found in sleep, but the sleep must be sound sleep: it must have quality as well as quantity.

To ensure sound sleep, the room must be quiet, dark and airy. The mattress must be smooth and straight, firm but resilient, the pillows neither too soft nor too hard, and the bedclothes warm but light.

If you sleep badly, check for constipation or indigestion. It is said that insomnia is often due to mild indigestion caused by a heavy or indigestible meal taken too near bedtime, or to some barely noticeable acidity. Try making the last meal of the day light and digestible, substituting a cup of peppermint tea or lime tisane for the possibly too stimulating tea or coffee.

Most cases of insomnia will react favourably to a warm bedtime bath. An excellent go-to-sleep bath is as follows: Use hot but not too hot water to which you have added a measure of pine-needle oil. Relax in the bath, dry slowly and without effort, then have a soothing drink and go straight to bed.

When you go to bed, think about relaxing rather than about sleeping and, in fact, refuse to let yourself go to sleep until every muscle in your body is completely relaxed. If you find this difficult, do a few relaxing exercises before your drink.

When the whole of your body is as relaxed as you can get it, it will begin to feel heavy and you won't want to move. That's fine – at bedtime! At other times, you may feel so comfortable and lethargic that you will want to drop off to sleep. If you have to get up and get going with other tasks and activities, be warned: your body is now working at a lower level, so take your time to return to normal. Never jump up quickly from relaxation – you might feel giddy. Clench and unclench your fists several times before you sit up, and sit up before you stand.

Relaxation

With practice, you can indulge yourself in a relaxation treatment whenever you like. You can do it lying on the floor or on the bed, or even sitting in a chair, although it does help if you can lie down. Stretch yourself out, close your eyes, let yourself go, and relax from your toes right up to the scalp and hair. Don't think of anything except your relaxing body. Relax your toes, feet, ankles, calves, knees, thighs and gradually, in your thoughts, come slowly up and up through your body until you reach the tips of your fingers, and lastly your hair. Keep going over in your mind – from feet to legs, from fingers to arms and then, lastly and most important, to face, scalp and hair.

If you have time to relax further, start to concentrate on your weight on the floor: feel the heels pressing hard on the ground – suddenly you feel your legs are like lead – then slowly the upper part of the body, the arms and the head, all feel heavy.

Still with eyes closed, concentrate on breathing in slowly through your nose and out through your mouth. Keep on breathing in and out very slowly until you feel that you are starting to float in the air, like a cloud floating in the sky.

Try to spare 10 to 15 minutes a day for this kind of mental exercise for your mind and body. You will feel wonderfully relaxed and content and your nervous system and body will have a new vitality.

When we deliberately relax our muscles, many other changes follow naturally. Blood pressure drops, heart beat and breathing slow down. The only trouble is that it isn't easy to learn to relax all the muscles in the body completely, and at will. Most people find it much easier to relax if they can lie in a really comfortable position, like one of the three illustrated on the opposite page.

You'll probably need a heap of pillows under your head and shoulders, and one for your knees. If you're skinny, you might need support under your elbows too. Experiment until you have found which position is best for you, wear loose comfortable clothing, and remove any hair accessories or chunky jewellery.

You must accept the fact that a woman's work is never done, not try to prove it false. You may be doing unnecessary jobs – never finding time to relax – because you have created rules you won't break. Monday is washing day, but one Monday you feel washed-out. Do you switch your timetable? All too often you struggle on with the chores and find that you are completely exhausted and miserable at the end of the day. Better to miss out and 'put your feet up' for a couple of hours – you will feel much better in the long run.

Lie on your right side. Extend your right leg and bend your left knee up. Bend your left arm so that your hand is on a level with your face, and relax your right arm behind you, palm up. Close your eyes and relax.

To rest and relieve aching or tired leg muscles and feet, lie for a few minutes with your feet on a pillow or book, to raise them slightly above your head.

Lie flat on your back with your arms by your sides, palms up. Let your arms and legs go limp and allow your feet to fall gently apart. Raise your chin, close your eyes and breathe deeply and regularly.

153

Yoga

It's easy to think of yoga, with its Indian origins, as a form of religion but that is not necessarily the case. Physical or Hatha Yoga is a series of well thought-through postures or poses that can benefit almost every part of the body. Not least of the merits of yoga are the relaxing properties. Many a woman under pressure would let everything else go by the board – lunch with a girl friend, a hair appointment, a shopping spree – rather than miss out on her yoga class.

Ideally, for the best possible introduction to yoga, go to a class; simple poses, however, can be practised at home. It is important to do each movement slowly and smoothly, and a good deal of practice is needed before some of the advanced poses can be attempted.

You should breathe slowly and deeply through the nose while doing yoga. Performing the movements correctly is priority: more detailed breathing instructions come into play when you are more advanced. Whether you practise for a few minutes or half an hour, concentrate completely on what you are doing. Shut out sounds, any distraction whatsoever.

One of the most relaxing exercises is to flop like a rag doll. Stand with your feet apart, arms at your sides. With your head and arms hanging, let your body bend forward as far as it will go. Count to 10, then slowly straighten up. With practice, your body will bend until your hands touch the floor. This exercise relaxes the head, neck, shoulders, arms, hands and back, and gently stretches the lower back and backs of the legs. Also, blood can flow to the head and this has a very refreshing effect.

Rolling the head is another very relaxing exercise which helps reduce tension in the neck and is very soothing to do. To avoid headaches and tensions, it is essential to keep the muscles and bones of the neck lubricated and free of settling toxins and poisons. You can do this exercise standing, but it's easier when sitting down, either on a chair or cross-legged on the floor. Do not attempt the Lotus position shown in the picture opposite: a good deal of practice will be necessary before you are able to hold this pose. For the time being, just sit with the legs comfortably crossed.

Head rolling: With eyes looking straight ahead, turn head to the left and hold for a couple of seconds. Roll the head round to the back and hold. Then roll the head around to the right and hold, before turning the face completely to the right with the chin raised. Drop the head forward, letting it feel heavy – be aware of the muscle pull on each side of the neck. Gently push the head down as you bring it round to the front again. Repeat once or twice in each direction.

To show how yoga can let you extend yourself without strain, here is an exercise which stretches and elongates the sides of the body, firming the torso as well as the legs and arms.

Stand with your feet well apart and your arms stretched sideways from the shoulders. Slowly bend to the left from your hips, keeping your right arm in line with your shoulder and holding your left knee with your left hand – both arms should be straight. Bring your right arm over, still straight and as close to your head as possible, and hold for a count of 5. Repeat on the other side. As you repeat this exercise, you will find that you can bring your arm over a little further until, eventually, it is parallel to the floor. You will be able to bend the supporting elbow so the body is brought over still further from the hips.

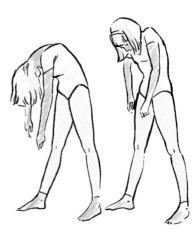

Stand with your feet apart, arms at your sides. With your head and arms hanging, let your body bend forward as far as it *will go. Count to 10, then slowly straighten up. With practice, your body will bend until your hands touch the floor.*

With eyes looking straight ahead, turn head to left. Hold for a couple of seconds. Roll the head round to the back and hold. Roll to the right and hold, before turning face completely to *the right with the chin raised. Drop the head forward, letting it feel heavy, then gently push head down as you bring it round to the front again. Repeat in the opposite direction.*

Stand with feet well apart, arms stretched sideways from the shoulders. Slowly bend to the left from the hips, keeping right arm in line with the shoulder and holding left knee with left hand – both arms should be straight. Bring right arm over, still straight and as close to the head as possible. Hold for a count of 5. Repeat on other side.

157

HEALTHY EATING

HEALTHY EATING

To maintain good health a well balanced diet is essential; i.e. one that provides adequate amounts of proteins, vitamins and minerals with the correct energy requirement – calories.

Each person varies in their requirements of nutrients and energy, and these change during their lifetime, i.e. during growth, pregnancy and breast feeding, and in old age. If certain nutrient needs are not met, this may lead to minor ailments, such as lethargy and poor complexion, whilst greater deficiency can lead to more serious illnesses, such as anaemia. Excess of certain foods can also be detrimental to health.

The Main Nutrients

Proteins: These provide the materials (amino acids) which are required for growth and repair of body cells. Some of the amino acids are classed as essential in that they cannot be produced in the body so have to be included in the diet. If there is an excessive intake of protein or a lack of calories, protein is broken down to provide energy. Protein can be provided by animal products, such as meat, fish, milk, eggs and cheese, and/or plant materials – cereals, nuts, beans, pulses and vegetables. Animal sources contain all the essential amino acids whereas plant materials may have one or more essential amino acids missing. This is overcome in vegetarian diets by mixing nuts, pulses and cereals so that the amino acids become balanced.

Fats: These provide a concentrated form of energy, i.e. they provide 9 calories/gm compared to proteins and carbohydrates which supply 4 calories/gm. Our diet consists of visible fats, such as butter, margarine, cooking fats, oils and fat on meat, and invisible fats, such as those in cakes, biscuits, nuts and lean meat.

Carbohydrates: These are also used to provide energy, and can be divided into:

Sugars – those naturally occurring in fruit, vegetables, plants and honey, and those that are refined into a concentrated form, such as table sugar, syrup, etc.

Starches – present in potatoes, bread, flour, cereal products, rice, pasta, etc. Starch is not as readily digestible as sugars but cooking makes it more so.

Cellulose and related substances – these form the fibrous structure of the cell walls of plants and are mostly indigestible

even after cooking. The fibrous bulk is essential in the diet for bowel functioning.

Vitamins: These are only required by the body in very small amounts. There are two groups of vitamins – fat soluble (A, D, E and K) and water soluble (B group and C). The fat soluble vitamins can be stored in the body whereas water soluble vitamins cannot and therefore have to be eaten every day.

Vitamin A – essential for vision in dim light, healthy skin and surface tissue. It is only found naturally in animal foods – especially liver, kidney, dairy produce and oily fish. The body can also obtain Vitamin A from carotene which is found in yellow and green vegetables. Another source is margarine which is fortified with vitamin A. Excessive intake of this vitamin is toxic.

Vitamin D – necessary for absorption of calcium and maintaining its level in the blood. Deficiency can lead to deficiency in calcium and hence rickets. Excessive intake can cause deposits of calcium in the kidneys (stones). Vitamin D can be produced by the action of sunlight on certain substances in the skin so dietary needs are small, except during pregnancy and lactation or if a person has little exposure to the sun. Dietary sources are oily fish, butter, and margarine which is enriched.

Vitamin E – the function of this is not fully understood but it is widespread in foods and a deficiency is unlikely.

Vitamin B group – these vitamins are required for the utilisation of energy.

Thiamin (B_1) – widely distributed in foods, rich sources being milk, offal, pork, eggs, vegetables, fruit, wholegrain cereals and fortified breakfast cereals.

Riboflavin (B_2) – widely distributed in foods. The main source in the UK being milk.

Nicotinic acid – there are many sources, the main ones being meat, fish, cheese and bread.

B_6 – used for the metabolism of amino acids. Occurs in meats, fish, eggs and wholegrain cereals.

B_{12} – needed for the production of blood and found only in animal foods, especially liver.

Folic acid – also needed for blood formation. Sources include offal, raw green leafy vegetables, pulses, bread, oranges.

Vitamin C – essential for healthy tissues. The main sources of vitamin C are fruit and vegetables. Care has to be taken because it is easily lost during storage, preparation and cooking.

Minerals: These control many bodily functions. Iron, calcium, phosphorus, magnesium, sodium, chlorine and potassium are the major minerals; others, such as fluoride, are required but only in trace amounts.

Iron – essential for blood. Deficiency causes anaemia. Sources in the diet include meat, especially offal, egs and vegetables.

Calcium – for bones, teeth and muscles. Sources in the diet are cheese, milk, bread and flour (which are fortified), and green vegetables.

Phosphorus – abundant in the body, and present in most foods.

Magnesium – in bones and all body cells. Widespread in food, especially vegetables.

Sodium and Chlorine – in all body fluids with the main source being salt. Usually consumed in excess of need.

Potassium – in body fluids. Sources include vegetables, fruit, meat and milk.

A Healthier Diet

Although malnutrition is quite rare in this country, problems arising from excesses of food are not and a large proportion of the population is overweight. Many diseases, such as diabetes, heart disease, high blood pressure and gall stones, are linked with overweight. For a healthier diet try to adapt your eating pattern as follows:

● Consume less fat – from both visible (butter, margarine, fats and oils, fat on meat) and invisible (cakes, biscuits, fried foods) sources. Obtain fat from vegetable sources rather than animal so that polyunsaturated fatty acid intake is increased at the expense of saturated fatty acids. Fat intake affects the cholesterol and lipoprotein levels in the blood which have been implicated with coronary heart disease.

● Eat less sugar – sugar is a carbohydrate source that provides only calories and *no* other nutrients. Sugar also encourages dental decay.

● Increase fibre intake – by eating wholemeal bread, wholegrain products, brown rice, bran products, beans, pulses, fruit and vegetables. Fibre has been shown to help in the prevention of bowel disorders, such as constipation and diverticulitis.

● Increase intake of fruit and vegetables – to provide fibre and carbohydrate in a form which also supplies vitamins and minerals (unlike sugar).

● Decrease salt intake – avoid eating too many highly salted processed foods. Reduce amount of salt added during cooking or at the table. High sodium levels can increase blood pressure, which is implicated in cerebro-vascular disease (stroke).

● Moderate alcohol intake. Alcohol provides a high number of calories with few other nutrients.

● Try the healthy menus and recipes on the following pages. They will be a good start in reshaping your eating habits.

FAMILY WINTER WEEKEND MENUS

SATURDAY

Breakfast: Dried Fruit Compote*
Sunflower Seed Bread* with Honey
Herb Tea

Lunch: Pizza
Cauliflower and Watercress Salad*
Bananas with Yogurt and Honey

Children's Tea: Jacket Potatoes Stuffed with Bacon and
Cheese
Carrot Salad
Prune and Apple Cake*

Parents' Dinner: Crudités with Avocado Mayonnaise
(sticks of raw vegetables served with
mayonnaise flavoured with 1 mashed
avocado, as a dip)
Chicken with Mushrooms*
Brown Rice
Green Salad
Apricot Wholemeal Crêpes*

SUNDAY

Breakfast: Apple Juice
Granola* with Yogurt
Wholemeal Bread with Honey
Herb Tea

Lunch: Roast Chicken with Herbs and Garlic
Potatoes Lyonnaise
(sliced potatoes and onions layered
in a dish and baked)
Brussels Sprouts
Wholemeal Blackberry Crumble*

High Tea: Toasted Sandwiches
Wholemeal Cheese Scones*
Wholemeal Sponge Cake*
Muesli Bars*

Recipes given on pages 167-173 and 186-189

FAMILY SUMMER WEEKEND MENUS

SATURDAY

Breakfast: Watermelon Compote
(cubes of melon flavoured with
honey and lemon juice)
Wholemeal Bread and Honey
Herb Tea

Picnic Lunch: Wholemeal Spinach Pie*
Tomato and Chive Salad
(thinly sliced tomatoes tossed in
Chive Dressing – see page 91)
Yogurt and Fresh Fruit

Children's Tea: Hamburgers in Wholemeal Buns
Green Salad
Apricot Slices*

Parents' Dinner: Tomato and Basil Soup*
Lamb Kebabs
(cubes of grilled lamb, onion, green
pepper and tomato)
Brown Rice
Green Salad
Strawberry and Yogurt Crunch*

SUNDAY

Breakfast: Banana Granola*
Wholemeal Bread and Honey
Herb Tea

Barbecue Lunch: Barbecued Chicken
Broccoli and Bean Sprout Salad*
Baked Potatoes with Soured Cream
Baked Bananas with Rum

Tea: Double Decker Sandwich
Wholemeal Cheese Scones*
Wholemeal Sponge Cake*

*Recipes given on pages 167-173 and 186-189

EVENING MEALS FOR SUMMER WEEKDAYS

Courgettes au Gratin*
Spinach and Mushroom Salad
Wholemeal Strawberry Sponge*

Grilled Trout with Herbs
Baby New Potatoes with Peas
Watermelon Sorbet*

Mushroom and Watercress Soup*
Salade Niçoise with crusty Wholemeal Bread
Fresh Fruit

Grilled Chicken with Herbs
New Potatoes
Spinach
Strawberries with Yogurt Snow*

Stuffed Aubergines*
Green Salad
Summer Fruit Salad*

EVENING MEALS FOR WINTER WEEKDAYS

Leek and Lentil Patties with Tomato Sauce*
Brown Rice
Baked Apples stuffed with Dates

Chicken and Red Pepper Pie*
Red Cabbage and Radish Salad*
Date and Apple Whip*

Vegetable Casserole*
Jacket Potatoes
Prune and Apple Cake*

Pear and Grape Vinaigrette*
Monkfish Américaine*
Brown Rice and Green Salad
Selection of Cheeses

Pork and Bean Ragoût*
Chinese Cabbage Salad
Fruit and Nut Salad*

*Recipes given on pages 167 -173 and 186-189

GRANOLA

120 ml (4 fl oz) safflower oil
90 ml (3 fl oz) malt extract
90 ml (3 fl oz) clear honey
250 g (8 oz) rolled oats
250 g (8 oz) jumbo oats
125 g (4 oz) hazelnuts
25 g (1 oz) desiccated coconut
50 g (2 oz) sunflower seeds
25 g (1 oz) sesame seeds

Place the oil, malt and honey in a large pan and heat gently until the malt is runny. Mix in the remaining ingredients and stir thoroughly.

Turn into a large roasting pan and bake in a preheated moderately hot oven, 190°C (375°F), Gas Mark 5, for 30 to 35 minutes, stirring occasionally so that it browns evenly. Allow to cool.

Store in an airtight container. Serve with natural yogurt.
MAKES ABOUT 1 KG (2 LB)

Banana Granola: Mix 125 g (4 oz) granola with 300 g (10.4 oz) natural yogurt and 1 sliced banana. SERVES 4.

DRIED FRUIT COMPOTE

250 g (8 oz) mixed dried fruits
50 g (2 oz) dried apricots
450 ml (¾ pint) apple juice

Place the dried fruits in a bowl with the apple juice and leave to soak overnight. Cover and simmer gently for 15 minutes, then pour into a serving bowl and cool.

Serve chilled, with yogurt.
SERVES 4

Fruit and Nut Salad: Simmer the fruit as above, adding 1 teaspoon ground cinnamon. Leave to cool, then add 2 sliced bananas and sprinkle with 25 g (1 oz) toasted flaked almonds.

MUSHROOM AND WATERCRESS SOUP

2 tablespoons olive oil
1 large onion, chopped
125 g (4 oz) button mushrooms,
  sliced
1 tablespoon flour
1 × 425 g (15 oz) can consommé
450 ml (¾ pint) water
1 bunch of watercress, chopped
salt and pepper

Heat the oil in a pan, add the onion and fry until softened. Add the mushrooms and fry for 2 minutes, then stir in the flour. Add the consommé, water, watercress,
and salt and pepper to taste; simmer for 10 minutes. Serve hot.
SERVES 4 TO 6.

COURGETTES AU GRATIN

3 tablespoons olive oil
2 onions, chopped
750 g (1½ lb) courgettes, sliced
2 cloves garlic, crushed
6 tomatoes, skinned and chopped
1 tablespoon tomato purée
2 tablespoons chopped parsley
salt and pepper
50 g (2 oz) wholemeal
  breadcrumbs
125 g (4 oz) Cheddar cheese, grated

Heat the oil in a pan, add the onions and courgettes and fry for 10 minutes, stirring occasionally. Add the garlic, tomatoes, tomato purée, parsley, and salt and pepper to taste. Cover and simmer for 15 to 20 minutes, then turn into a 1.5 litre (2½ pint) ovenproof dish.

Mix the breadcrumbs with the cheese and sprinkle over the courgettes to cover completely. Brown under a preheated hot grill for about 5 minutes.
SERVES 4

LEEK AND LENTIL PATTIES

3 tablespoons olive oil
2 leeks, thinly sliced
2 celery sticks, chopped
250 g (8 oz) brown lentils
600 ml (1 pint) water
1 tablespoon soy sauce
salt and pepper
2 tablespoons chopped parsley
125 g (4 oz) wholemeal
  breadcrumbs
oil for shallow-frying
TOMATO SAUCE:
1 × 397 g (14 oz) can tomatoes
2 cloves garlic
1 tablespoon chopped parsley
1 bay leaf

Heat the oil in a pan, add the leeks and celery and fry slowly until softened, stirring occasionally. Add the lentils, water, soy sauce, and salt and pepper to taste and bring to the boil. Cover and simmer for 50 minutes to 1 hour, stirring occasionally. Mix in the parsley and half the breadcrumbs; turn onto a plate to cool.

With wet hands, shape the mixture into 12 patties and coat with remaining breadcrumbs.

Pour oil into a frying pan to a depth of 5 mm (¼ inch) and place over a moderate heat. When hot, add the patties and fry until crisp and golden brown, turning once.

To make the sauce, place the tomatoes with their juice in a pan, stirring well to break up the tomatoes. Add the remaining ingredients, with salt and pepper to taste, and simmer for 15 minutes. Serve with the patties.

SERVES 4

CHICKEN AND RED PEPPER PIE

2 tablespoons oil
1 onion, chopped
1 clove garlic, crushed
50 g (2 oz) mushrooms, sliced
3 celery sticks, sliced
1 red pepper, cored, seeded and
  sliced
1 tablespoon flour
300 ml (½ pint) chicken stock
500 g (1 lb) cooked chicken,
  shredded
salt and pepper
250 g (8 oz) wholemeal pastry (see
  opposite page)
beaten egg to glaze

Heat the oil in a pan, add the onion and fry until softened. Add the garlic, mushrooms, celery and red pepper and cook for 5 to 8 minutes, stirring occasionally. Remove from the heat and stir in the flour. Pour in the stock and stir until blended. Return to the heat and bring to the boil, stirring, until thickened. Stir in the chicken, and salt and pepper to taste. Transfer to a 1.2 litre (2 pint) pie dish and leave to cool.

Roll out the pastry to a shape about 5 cm (2 inches) larger than the dish. Cut off a narrow strip all round and place on the dampened edge of the dish. Dampen the strip then cover with the pastry, sealing well. Trim and flute the edges, decorate with pastry leaves made from the trimmings and make a hole in the centre. Brush with egg and bake in a preheated moderately hot oven, 200°C (400°F), Gas Mark 6, for 30 minutes. Serve hot.

SERVES 4

PORK AND BEAN RAGOÛT

4 tablespoons oil
350 g (12 oz) lean pork, cut into
  2.5 cm (1 inch) cubes
2 onions, sliced
350 g (12 oz) black beans, soaked
  overnight and drained
750 ml (1¼ pints) water
2 celery sticks
2 cloves garlic, crushed
1 × 397 g (14 oz) can tomatoes
1 bay leaf
1 red pepper, cored, seeded and
  chopped
2 tablespoons chopped parsley
salt and pepper

Heat half the oil in a flameproof casserole, add the meat and fry briskly until sealed. Remove from the pan and set aside. Heat the remaining oil, then add the onions and fry until softened. Add the beans and water, cover, bring to the boil and simmer for 30 minutes.

Return the meat to the pan with the celery, garlic, tomatoes with their juice and bay leaf. Cover and cook in a preheated moderate oven, 180°C (350°F), Gas Mark 4, for 45 minutes.

Stir in the red pepper, parsley, and salt and pepper to taste, then return to the oven for 30 minutes, until the beans are soft.
SERVES 4

WHOLEMEAL SPINACH PIE

PASTRY:
350 g (12 oz) wholemeal flour
1 teaspoon salt
175 g (6 oz) margarine or butter
3-4 tablespoons iced water
beaten egg to glaze
FILLING:
2 tablespoons olive oil
1 large onion, chopped
2 cloves garlic, crushed
4 × 227 g (8 oz) packets frozen
  chopped spinach, slightly thawed
1 egg, beaten
½ teaspoon grated nutmeg
50 g (2 oz) grated Parmesan cheese
salt and pepper

First prepare the filling. Heat the oil in a pan, add the onion and fry until softened. Add the garlic and spinach, cover and cook gently for 10 minutes, stirring occasionally. Remove the lid and cook for a further 5 minutes. Cool slightly, then beat in the egg, nutmeg, cheese, and salt and pepper to taste. Cool completely.

Meanwhile, make the pastry as for Apricot slices (see page 171). Cut off two thirds of the dough, roll out thinly on a floured surface and use to line a 23 cm (9 inch) shallow pie plate.

Turn the filling into the prepared dish and spread evenly. Dampen the pastry edges. Roll out the remaining pastry thinly and place in position for the lid, sealing well. Trim and flute the edges, decorate with pastry leaves made from the trimmings and make a hole in the centre. Chill for 15 minutes. Brush with beaten egg and bake in a preheated moderately hot oven, 200°C (400°F), Gas Mark 6, for 45 to 50 minutes.

Serve hot or cold with a salad.
SERVES 6

STUFFED AUBERGINES

2 large aubergines
2 tablespoons olive oil
1 large onion, chopped
2 cloves garlic, crushed
250 g (8 oz) mushrooms, sliced
50 g (2 oz) brown rice, cooked
2 tablespoons tomato purée
50 g (2 oz) cashew nuts, chopped
2 tablespoons chopped parsley
salt and pepper
75 g (3 oz) Cheddar cheese, grated

Prick the aubergines all over with a fork, cut in half and place cut side down on a greased baking sheet. Bake in a preheated moderately hot oven, 190°C (375°F), Gas Mark 5, for 30 minutes.

Meanwhile, heat the oil in a pan, add the onion and fry until softened. Add the garlic and mushrooms and fry over a gentle heat for 3 minutes. Add the rice, tomato purée, nuts, parsley, and salt and pepper to taste. Mix well and heat through gently while preparing the aubergines.

Scoop the flesh from the aubergines, without breaking the skin, chop finely and mix with the rice mixture. Pile into the aubergine skins, sprinkle with the cheese and bake for 10 minutes, until the cheese has melted.
SERVES 4

APRICOT WHOLEMEAL CRÊPES

BATTER:
125 g (4 oz) wholemeal flour
1 egg
300 ml (½ pint) milk
1 tablespoon oil
FILLING:
250 g (8 oz) dried apricots, chopped
  and soaked for 2 hours
2 teaspoons arrowroot
1 tablespoon clear honey
TO FINISH:
2 tablespoons clear honey
25 g (1 oz) flaked almonds, toasted
TO SERVE:
Yogurt snow (see page 189)

Place the flour, egg and milk in an electric blender or food processor and work for 30 seconds, until the batter is smooth.

Heat a 15 cm (6 inch) omelet pan and add 1 teaspoon of the oil. When hot, pour in 1 tablespoon of the batter and tilt the pan to coat the bottom evenly. Cook until the underside is brown, then turn and cook for 10 seconds. Repeat with the remaining batter, stacking the pancakes as they cook.

To make the filling, place the apricots and their soaking liquid in a pan, cover and simmer for 10 minutes. Mix the arrowroot with a little water, stir into the apricots with the honey and cook, stirring, until thickened.

Place a little filling on each pancake, roll up and arrange in an ovenproof dish.

Warm the honey and spoon over the pancakes to glaze. Place in a preheated moderate oven, 180°C (350°F), Gas Mark 4, for 10 to 15 minutes, until heated through. Sprinkle with the almonds and serve with the Yogurt snow.
SERVES 4

WHOLEMEAL BLACKBERRY CRUMBLE

175 g (6 oz) wholemeal flour
75 g (3 oz) margarine
125 g (4 oz) raw sugar
50 g (2 oz) hazelnuts, chopped
350 g (12 oz) dessert apples, peeled and cored
350 g (12 oz) blackberries

Place the flour in a mixing bowl and rub in the margarine until the mixture resembles breadcrumbs. Stir in 75 g (3 oz) of the sugar and the hazelnuts.

Slice the apples and mix with the blackberries and remaining sugar. Turn into a 900 ml (1½ pint) pie dish and sprinkle the crumble over the fruit to cover it completely.

Bake in a preheated moderate oven, 180°C (350°F), Gas Mark 4, for 40 to 50 minutes, until golden brown.

Serve hot or cold, with natural yogurt sweetened with honey.
SERVES 4 TO 6

APRICOT SLICES

250 g (8 oz) wholemeal flour
125 g (4 oz) margarine or butter
2-3 tablespoons water
FILLING:
125 g (4 oz) margarine or butter
75 g (3 oz) raw sugar
2 eggs
50 g (2 oz) wholemeal flour
175 g (6 oz) dried apricots, chopped and soaked for 2 hours
125 g (4 oz) ground almonds
½ teaspoon almond essence
50 g (2 oz) flaked almonds

Place the flour in a mixing bowl and rub in the fat until the mixture resembles breadcrumbs. Stir in enough water to mix to a firm dough. Turn onto a floured surface and knead lightly. Roll out thinly and use to line a 30 × 20 cm (12 × 8 inch) Swiss roll tin. Chill for 15 minutes.

Meanwhile, cream the fat and sugar together until fluffy, then beat in the eggs one at a time, adding half the flour with each one. Drain the apricots and dry on kitchen paper. Stir into the mixture with the ground almonds and essence. Place in the prepared tin and smooth evenly to the edges. Sprinkle the almonds on top.

Bake in a preheated moderately hot oven, 190°C (375°F), Gas Mark 5, for 40 to 45 minutes, until golden. Cool in the tin for a few minutes, then place carefully on a wire rack to cool completely. Cut into slices to serve.
MAKES 18

MUESLI BARS

125 g (4 oz) butter or margarine
90 ml (3 fl oz) clear honey
350 g (12 oz) muesli
2 tablespoons sesame seeds

Place the fat and honey in a large pan and heat gently until melted. Stir in the muesli and sesame seeds and mix thoroughly.

Turn into a greased 18 × 28 cm (7 × 11 inch) baking tin and smooth the top with a wet palette knife.

Bake in a preheated moderate oven, 180°C (350°F), Gas Mark 4, for 20 to 25 minutes.

Cool in the tin for 2 minutes, then cut into bars. Cool for a further 15 minutes, then remove from the tin.
MAKES 16

NOTE: The sweetness of these bars will depend on the type of muesli used. If liked, add 1 to 2 tablespoons raw sugar.

PRUNE AND APPLE CAKE

125 g (4 oz) stoned prunes, chopped
150 ml (¼ pint) water
125 g (4 oz) soft brown sugar
120 ml (4 fl oz) corn oil
2 eggs
150 g (5 oz) wholemeal flour
½ teaspoon bicarbonate of soda
1 teaspoon ground mixed spice
1 teaspoon ground cinnamon
120 ml (4 fl oz) natural yogurt
1 dessert apple, cored and grated
25 g (1 oz) walnuts, chopped

Grease a 20 cm (8 inch) deep cake tin, line the base with grease-proof paper and grease again.

Place the prunes in a pan with the water, cover and simmer gently for 10 minutes. Stir in the sugar and allow to cool.

Stir in the remaining ingredients, except the walnuts, and beat together thoroughly. Pour the mixture into the prepared tin and sprinkle the walnuts on top.

Bake in a preheated moderate oven, 180°C (350°F), Gas Mark 4, for 30 minutes, until firm to the touch.

Remove from the tin and peel off the lining paper. Serve hot as a dessert, or cold as a cake.

SERVES 6 TO 8

WHOLEMEAL CHEESE SCONES

125 g (4 oz) wholemeal flour
125 g (4 oz) plain flour
1 teaspoon cream of tartar
½ teaspoon bicarbonate of soda
½ teaspoon salt
pinch of cayenne pepper
1 teaspoon dry mustard
50 g (2 oz) butter or margarine
125 g (4 oz) Cheddar cheese, grated
120 ml (4 fl oz) milk
(approximately)

Place the wholemeal flour in a mixing bowl, then sift in the plain flour and remaining dry ingredients. Rub in the fat until the mixture resembles bread-crumbs, then stir in 75 g (3 oz) of the cheese and enough milk to mix to a soft dough.

Turn onto a floured surface, knead lightly and roll out to a 2 cm (¾ inch) thickness. Cut into 5 cm (2 inch) rounds with a plain cutter and place on a floured baking sheet. Sprinkle with the remaining cheese.

Bake in a preheated moderately hot oven, 200°C (400°F), Gas Mark 6, for 15 minutes. Transfer to a wire rack to cool. Serve split and buttered.

MAKES 10

WHOLEMEAL SPONGE CAKE

2 eggs
75 g (3 oz) soft brown sugar
1 teaspoon ground cinnamon
50 g (2 oz) wholemeal flour
1 tablespoon corn oil
FILLING:
1 tablespoon clear honey
2 tablespoons apple juice
½ teaspoon ground cinnamon
3 dessert apples, cored and sliced

Line the base of a 20 cm (8 inch) sandwich tin, then grease and flour.

Whisk the eggs and sugar together in an electric blender or food processor until thick and mousse-like. Sift the cinnamon into the flour, then carefully fold into the whisked mixture with a metal spoon. Fold in the oil, then turn into the prepared tin.

Bake in a preheated moderately hot oven, 190°C (375°F), Gas Mark 5, for 20 to 25 minutes, until the cake springs back when lightly pressed. Turn onto a wire rack to cool.

To make the filling, place the honey and apple juice in a heavy-based pan. Add the cinnamon and apples, cover and simmer gently for 5 minutes, stirring occasionally. Leave in the pan until cold.

Split the cake in half horizontally and sandwich together with the filling.

MAKES ONE 20 CM (8 INCH) CAKE

VARIATIONS:
Whisk 4 tablespoons double cream and spread over the cake and top with the filling.
Wholemeal Strawberry Sponge: Whisk 142 ml (5 fl oz) double cream, fold in 125 g (4 oz) sliced strawberries and 1 teaspoon clear honey and use to sandwich the cakes together.

SUNFLOWER SEED BREAD

750 g (1½ lb) wholemeal flour
750 g (1½ lb) granary flour
3 teaspoons salt
75 g (3 oz) sunflower seeds
25 g (1 oz) fresh yeast
900 ml-1.2 litres (1½-2 pints)
   warm water
2 tablespoons malt extract
2 tablespoons sunflower oil

Mix the flours, salt and all but 2 tablespoons of the sunflower seeds together in a mixing bowl. Chop the reserved sunflower seeds and set aside. Cream the yeast with a little of the water and leave until frothy. Add to the flour mixture with the remaining water, malt extract and oil; mix to a soft dough.

Turn onto a floured surface and knead for 5 minutes until smooth and elastic. Place in a bowl, cover with a damp cloth and leave to rise in a warm place for about 1½ hours until doubled in size.

Turn onto a floured surface and knead for a few minutes, then divide into 4 pieces. Shape and place each piece in a greased 500 g/1 lb loaf tin. Brush with water and sprinkle with the chopped sunflower seeds.

Cover loosely and leave to rise in a warm place for about 30 minutes until the dough just reaches the top of the tins. Bake in a preheated hot oven, 220°C (425°F), Gas Mark 7, for 15 minutes. Lower the temperature to 190°C (375°F), Gas Mark 5, and bake for a further 20 minutes or until the bread sounds hollow when tapped. Turn onto a wire rack to cool.

MAKES FOUR 500 G (1 LB) LOAVES

SLIMMING

SLIMMING

At the present time approximately 40% of the adult population is overweight and there is an increasing number of children who are overweight. We become overweight when our intake of calories is greater than those used, so the excess is converted to fat and stored in the body. The solution to this problem is to reduce the number of calories taken in and increase activity to use more calories. Increasing activity alone is not very successful because each pound of fat represents 3,500 calories which would mean hours of exercise!

'Crash' diets – where only very few calories are taken in usually as one or two foods – are not very wise because they can only be maintained for a short time. They can be dangerous, in that they affect the metabolic balance of the body, and are usually not very successful because the main weight loss is due to body fluid not fat. If this type of diet is prolonged, the body's protein-rich stores start to break down, i.e. muscles. It is much wiser to aim at losing about 1 kg (2 lb) a week which requires a reduction of about 1,000 calories a day.

The body requires at least 800-1,000 calories per day for ordinary functioning so for weight reduction there should be a calorie intake of: 1,000-1,200 for women and 1,200-1,500 for men. Anyone reducing the amount of food they are eating must keep a close check that their requirements for proteins, vitamins, minerals and fibre are met. Anyone who has a known medical condition or is taking some form of medication should always seek the advice of a doctor or dietician before commencing any diet.

Some Useful Hints to Help Dieting

- Weigh yourself once a week only, on the same day, at the same time, preferably without clothes and using the same scales. The scales must be accurate. To check, place a fixed, known weight on the centre, take the reading and adjust if necessary. Move your scales as little as possible.
- Try to have three meals a day with a protein food at each meal.
- Always sit down at a table and eat food with a knife and fork.
- Don't eat snacks between meals. If really necessary have an extra drink – water, tea, coffee, bovril, oxo, lemon juice – or eat a piece of fruit, a tomato, or a stick of celery.
- Take in plenty of fluids.

Calorie controlled diets

You can count all your calorie intake by weighing all of the food you eat. Alternatively you should be able to cut calories by following this plan:

Eat average helpings of:

Lean meat – about 125 g (4 oz)	Beef, veal, pork, lamb, rabbit, liver, kidney, bacon, ham, chicken, etc (lean only).
Fish – about 150 g (5 oz)	All types including shellfish.
Eggs	Boiled or poached (1 egg); scrambled or as a small omelet (2 eggs).
Cheese – 25-50 g (1-2 oz)	All except cream cheese.

Eat or drink as much as you like of:

Vegetables	Cabbage, cauliflower, French or runner beans, broccoli, kale, spinach, Brussels sprouts, etc.
Salads	Lettuce, tomato, celery, radish, cucumber, etc.
Fresh fruit	Apples, oranges, pears, grapes.
Seasonings	Vinegar, herbs, spices.
Drinks	Water, soda water, sugar-free drinks, pure lemon juice, tea and coffee without sugar and using milk from the daily allowance.
Sweetener	Liquid or tablet low-calorie sweeteners.

Do NOT eat:

Sugary foods	Sugar, sweets, chocolates, ice-cream, cakes, biscuits, jams, jellies, marmalade, honey, lemon curd, tinned fruit in syrup, milk drinks, drinking chocolate and flavoured yogurt.
Starchy foods	Cakes, biscuits, pasta foods, semolina, rice, pies, thickened sauces, custard.
Fatty foods	All fried foods, meat fat, sausages, nuts, crisps, cooking oils and fats, salad dressing, mayonnaise, cream, evaporated and condensed milk, cream cheese.
Drinks	All containing sugar, glucose or alcohol, e.g. lager, beer, wine, liqueurs, fizzy drinks, Lucozade, squash, sweetened fruit juice, Ribena, malted and bedtime drinks.

Adhere to daily and weekly allowances of butter, margarine, milk and bread.

An outline of a calorie controlled diet
Butter or margarine – 125 g (4 oz) per week – to supply vitamin A and D requirements.
Milk – 200-300 ml (⅓-½ pint) milk or 400-600 ml (⅔-1 pint) skimmed milk per day.
Bread – 3 large thin slices of wholemeal bread per day.

Breakfast
½ grapefruit
1 egg, poached or boiled
2 tomatoes
1 slice wholemeal bread
(from daily allowance)

Mid-day meal
Average helping of lean meat
or fish or egg or cheese
Plenty of steamed or boiled
vegetables or salad
2 slices wholemeal bread
(from daily allowance)
1 apple

Evening meal
Average helping of lean meat
or fish or egg or cheese
Plenty of steamed or boiled
vegetables or salad
1-2 boiled or jacket potatoes
(the size of an egg)
1 orange

Children require more calories and vitamins because of growth so allow 600 ml (1 pint) milk and more fruit and vegetables. Men require more calories so allow an extra 1 or 2 slices of bread and 1 or 2 potatoes and more fruit and vegetables.

SUMMER CALORIE CONTROLLED DIET PLAN

	Monday	Tuesday	Wednesday	Thursday	Friday	Saturday	Sunday
Breakfast	1 small glass unsweetened fruit juice 2 tbsp muesli with milk	½ grapefruit 1 poached egg 1 slice bread	fresh fruit in 150 g (5 oz) natural low fat yogurt 1 slice bread	1 small glass unsweetened fruit juice 1 boiled egg 1 slice bread	½ grapefruit 25 g (1 oz) cheese on 1 slice toast	1 small glass unsweetened fruit juice 2 tbsp branflakes with milk	½ grapefruit 2 rashers lean bacon, grilled 2 tomatoes 1 slice bread
Light meal	125 g (4 oz) lean meat salad 2 slices bread 1 nectarine	1 × 150 g (5 oz) smoked mackerel fillet salad 2 slices toast cherries	25 g (1 oz) cheese salad 2 slices bread 1 small bunch grapes	125 g (4 oz) cottage cheese tomato cucumber 2 slices bread 3 plums	125 g (4 oz) roast chicken salad 2 slices bread 4-6 strawberries	tomatoes stuffed with 125 g (4 oz) cottage cheese salad 2 slices bread 1 peach	125 g (4 oz) ham salad 2 slices bread 1 slice melon
Main meal	1 slice melon 150 g (5 oz) mixed shellfish salad 1 slice bread strawberries and raspberries with 150 g (5 oz) natural low fat yogurt	Pear & Grape Vinaigrette* 2-egg omelet seasonal vegetables 1-2 new potatoes Lemon sorbet	Grapefruit cocktail 125 g (4 oz) Tandoori chicken piece 2 tbsp brown rice salad 1 peach	Vichyssoise 125 g (4 oz) roast meat 1-2 new potatoes seasonal vegetables Summer Fruit Salad*	Florida cocktail 150 g (5 oz) tuna fish (canned in brine) salad 1 slice bread natural low fat yogurt with 1 tbsp muesli	1 small glass unsweetened fruit juice 125 g (4 oz) cold roast beef Broccoli and Bean sprout Salad* 1 slice bread Watermelon Sorbet*	Tomato and Basil Soup* 125 g (4 oz) grilled liver rice green salad Strawberry and Yogurt Crunch*

NOTE: All bread and milk must be taken from the daily allowance; all butter or margarine must be taken from the weekly allowance. These are given on page 179. Recipes marked with an asterisk are given on pages 186-189.

WINTER CALORIE CONTROLLED DIET PLAN

	Monday	Tuesday	Wednesday	Thursday	Friday	Saturday	Sunday
Breakfast	1 small glass unsweetened fruit juice 3 tbsp branflakes with milk	½ grapefruit 1 boiled egg 1 slice wholemeal bread	2 tbsp muesli with milk 1 slice toast 2 tomatoes	½ grapefruit 2 rashers lean bacon, grilled 2 tomatoes 1 slice toast	1 small glass unsweetened fruit juice 1 poached egg 2 tbsp baked beans	3 tbsp porridge with milk fresh fruit	1 small glass unsweetened fruit juice 150 g (5 oz) kipper with grilled mushrooms 1 slice bread
Light meal	2 slices cheese on toast, using 25 g (1 oz) cheese 1 apple	cauliflower with 50 g (2 oz) melted cheese 1 slice bread 1 orange	1 poached egg on vegetables 1 slice bread 1 apple	150 g (5 oz) canned salmon salad 1 banana	150 g (5 oz) any smoked fish 2 tbsps brown rice, cooked 1 pear	2 tbsps baked beans on 1 slice toast 1 orange	2-egg omelet 2 tomatoes 1 slice bread 1 pear
Main meal	Mushroom and Watercress soup* Monkfish Américaine* 1 boiled potato vegetables Dried fruit compote	Tomato and Basil Soup* 150 g (5 oz) any poached white fish 2 tbsps brown rice, cooked Date and Apple Whip*	150 g (5 oz) natural low fat yogurt with cucumber 125 g (4 oz) grilled liver 2 tbsps brown rice, cooked Poached pears	½ grapefruit Vegetable Casserole* 2 slices bread 150 g (5 oz) natural low fat yogurt with 25 g (1 oz) nuts	Onion soup 175 g (6 oz) pork chop, grilled 1 jacket potato red cabbage Stewed fruit	Pear & Grape Vinaigrette* Chicken with Mushrooms* 1–2 boiled potatoes vegetables fresh fruit	Grapefruit cocktail 125 g (4 oz) roast turkey 1–2 boiled potatoes Cauliflower and Watercress Salad* Baked apple

NOTE: All bread and milk must be taken from the daily allowance; all butter or margarine must be taken from the weekly allowance. These are given on page 179. Recipes marked with an asterisk are given on pages 186-189.

181

Alternative Diets

People often say they cannot keep to a calorie controlled diet because they can't be bothered to count the calories. Other diets which will help reduce weight are ones that restrict certain foods.

Low Carbohydrate Diet

Instead of considering calories, try to keep carbohydrates to: 60-100 g (2-3.5 oz) per day for women and 105-120 g (3.7-4.2 oz) per day for men and children.

To reduce carbohydrate, exclude sugar and starchy foods, i.e. sugar, biscuits, cakes, bread, cereals, rice, noodles, spaghetti, savoury snacks, sugary beverages, alcoholic drinks, jams, honey, sweets, thick sauces, soups, puddings, ice-cream.

Foods that can be eaten without limit are lean meat, sausages, fish, eggs, cheese, salads, vegetables, fresh fruit, canned fruit in natural juice, nuts as part of a main meal.

High quantities of protein tend to be eaten in this type of diet; as protein is very satisfying, this helps limit food intake.

Even in a low carbohydrate diet you are allowed 300 ml (½ pint) milk, 15 g (½ oz) butter or margarine, up to 75 g (3 oz) bread and one small helping of cereal product, i.e. rice, spaghetti, cereal, each day.

Here are suggestions for different breakfasts, light meals and main meals. Make up your own menu plans from the choices given below; any variations will still keep you within the recommended limits of carbohydrate intake. All bread, milk and butter or margarine (used for spreading or cooking) must be taken from the daily allowance.

Breakfast
1 small glass tomato juice
or ½ grapefruit
plus 1 egg, poached or boiled
or 1-2 rashers lean grilled bacon
or 125 g (4 oz) kipper fillet
plus 1 crispbread

Light meal
2-egg omelet and salad
or
125 g (4 oz) piece chicken
plus salad
or 125 g (4 oz) tuna
(canned in brine) plus salad
plus 1 piece of citrus fruit
or 1 wedge of melon

Main meal
Tomato and Basil Soup★
or Pear and Grape Vinaigrette★
or ½ grapefruit
plus Vegetable Casserole★ (no potato)
or 175 g (6 oz) pork chop, grilled, plus vegetables and 1-2 small boiled potatoes
or 125 g (4 oz) piece golden haddock, plus 1 poached egg, vegetables and 1 slice wholemeal bread
plus stewed fruit (using low calorie sweetener)
or ½ low fat natural yogurt
or Fresh raspberries and strawberries

Low Fat Diet

In a low fat diet try to reduce the fat intake in the diet. You are still allowed 50 g (2 oz) butter or margarine or 125 g (4 oz) low fat spread per week; this is to ensure adequate intake of vitamins A and D (or a vitamin supplement is necessary). Also allowed is 150 ml (¼ pint) milk or 300 ml (½ pint) skimmed milk, and a maximum of 1 egg per day.

Foods not allowed include: all fried foods, oils and fats, cakes, biscuits, cream, hard cheese, fried snacks such as crisps, high fat content meat products such as pork pie, sausages, salami, etc.

Foods allowed include: lean meat (all visible fat trimmed off), poultry with the skin removed, fish, canned fish in brine (not oil), cottage cheese, bread, rice, spaghetti, pasta, potatoes, and any quantity of fruit and vegetables.

Make up your own menu plans from the choices given below. Bread, milk and butter or margarine (used for spreading or cooking) must be taken from the daily/weekly allowance.

Breakfast
½ grapefruit
or 1 small glass of unsweetened fruit juice
plus 2 tablespoons wheatflakes or branflakes or cornflakes
plus 150 ml (¼ pint) milk
or 1 boiled or poached egg, plus 1 slice wholemeal bread
or 1 rasher of lean bacon, grilled, plus 1 slice wholemeal bread

Light meal
125 g (4 oz) cottage cheese, plus salad and 1 slice wholemeal bread
or 2 tablespoons baked beans on 1 slice wholemeal bread, toasted
or 125 g (4 oz) tuna (canned in brine), plus salad
plus 1 piece of fruit

Main meal
Tomato and Basil Soup★
or 1 wedge of melon
plus Vegetable Casserole★
or 125 g (4 oz) roast chicken (no skin), plus vegetables including 1-2 boiled potatoes
or 150 g (5 oz) poached haddock, plus vegetables including 1-2 boiled potatoes
plus Watermelon Sorbet★
or Fresh fruit
or Stewed fruit

High Fibre Reducing Diet

A high fibre diet makes a useful healthy slimming diet. High fibre foods generally need a lot of chewing so you feel you are eating more but – more important – high fibre foods are bulky so the stomach feels satisfied more quickly.

The basic principles of a calorie controlled diet still hold for a high fibre diet so sweet and sugary foods should be avoided, starchy foods should be restricted, and fatty foods avoided. To

increase your fibre intake and reduce calorie intake:
- Substitute wholemeal breakfast cereals for refined cereals. Use Bran Flakes, All Bran, Wheat Flakes, Wholewheat Biscs, porridge.
- Replace white or brown bread with 100% wholemeal bread or Ryvita or brown crispbreads.
- Limit butter and margarine to 125 g (4 oz) maximum per week.
- Have no more than 300 ml (½ pint) milk or 600 ml (1 pint) skimmed milk per day.
- Eat plenty of fruit and vegetables, particularly with the skin and peel on, e.g. jacket potatoes, baked apples. Never peel eating apples or pears.
- Supplement your diet with unprocessed bran by sprinkling a spoonful on cereals, soups, gravy, drinks, vegetables and stewed fruit.
- Use wholemeal spaghetti and pasta.
- Use brown rice.

Make up your own high fibre menu plans from the choices given below, keeping to milk and butter/margarine allowances.

Breakfast
½ grapefruit
or 1 small glass unsweetened fruit juice
plus 2 tablespoons Bran Flakes plus 1 tablespoon bran and 150 ml (¼ pint) milk
or 2 tablespoons muesli plus 1 tablespoon bran and 150 ml (¼ pint) milk
or 1 poached or boiled egg plus 1 slice wholemeal bread

Light meal
2 tablespoons baked beans on 1 slice wholemeal bread, toasted
or 2 slices wholemeal bread, plus 25 g (1 oz) grated cheese and salad
or 50 g (2 oz) wholewheat macaroni cheese, made with cornflour, 150 ml (¼ pint) milk and 25 g (1 oz) cheese
plus 1 banana
or 125 g (4 oz) raspberries

Main meal
Lentil soup
or Pea and ham soup
or 1 tomato stuffed with 50 g (2 oz) cottage cheese
plus Monkfish Américaine* plus 50 g (2 oz) wholemeal spaghetti
or Vegetable Casserole* (with kidney beans and 1 tablespoon bran added)
or 125 g (4 oz) grilled gammon steak, plus broad beans or peas and 1 jacket potato
plus 50 g (2 oz) stewed dried fruits (apricots and prunes)
or 150 g (5 oz) natural low fat yogurt with 25 g (1 oz) nuts and 1 tablespoon bran
or Stewed fruit with 1 tablespoon bran

PEAR AND GRAPE VINAIGRETTE

3 tablespoons Chive dressing (see opposite page)
2 ripe dessert pears, peeled and cored
175 g (6 oz) black grapes, halved and seeded
2 oranges, peeled and cut into segments
1 tablespoon sesame seeds, toasted

Place the dressing in a mixing bowl. Slice the pears into the dressing and coat thoroughly. Add the grapes and oranges and toss together. Spoon into individual serving bowls and sprinkle with the sesame seeds to serve.
SERVES 4 TO 6
Calories per portion: 110

TOMATO AND BASIL SOUP

500 g (1 lb) tomatoes, skinned and roughly chopped
1 clove garlic
300 ml (½ pint) water
300 ml (½ pint) tomato juice
salt and pepper
1 tablespoon basil, chopped

Place the tomatoes, garlic and water in an electric blender or food processor and work for 30 seconds until smooth. Pour into a tureen, stir in the tomato juice and season liberally with salt and pepper. Mix in half the basil and chill well. Sprinkle with the remaining basil to serve.
SERVES 6
Calories per portion: 21

RED CABBAGE AND RADISH SALAD

2 red dessert apples, quartered and cored
350 g (12 oz) red cabbage, shredded
1 bunch of radishes, thinly sliced
HONEY AND LEMON DRESSING:
2 tablespoons lemon juice
2 tablespoons clear honey
2 tablespoons apple juice
1 tablespoon chopped parsley
salt and pepper

Put all the dressing ingredients, with salt and pepper to taste, in a screw-topped jar and shake well. Pour into a salad bowl.
   Slice the apples into the dressing. Add cabbage and radishes, toss well and marinate for 1 to 2 hours, tossing occasionally. Toss again just before serving.
SERVES 6
Calories per portion: 80

CAULIFLOWER AND WATERCRESS SALAD

1 small cauliflower, broken into florets
salt and pepper
1 bunch of watercress
YOGURT DRESSING:
4 tablespoons natural yogurt
1 tablespoon lemon juice
1 clove garlic, crushed
1 teaspoon clear honey
1 tablespoon chopped parsley

Blanch the cauliflower in boiling salted water for 3 minutes. Drain and leave to cool. Place in a salad bowl with the watercress.
   Put the dressing ingredients in a screw-topped jar, adding salt and pepper to taste; shake well. Pour over the salad just before serving and toss thoroughly.
SERVES 6
Calories per portion: 40

BROCCOLI AND BEAN SPROUT SALAD

250 g (8 oz) broccoli, broken into
florets
salt and pepper
175 g (6 oz) bean sprouts
1 small red pepper, cored, seeded
and sliced
2 tablespoons sesame seeds, toasted
CHIVE DRESSING:
2 tablespoons olive oil
2 teaspoons cider vinegar
1/2 teaspoon clear honey
1/2 teaspoon Dijon mustard
2 tablespoons chopped chives

Blanch the broccoli in boiling salted water for 4 minutes. Drain and leave to cool. Place in a salad bowl with the bean sprouts, red pepper and sesame seeds.

Put all the dressing ingredients, with salt and pepper to taste, in a screw-topped jar and shake well. Pour over the salad and toss thoroughly to serve.

SERVES 4
Calories per portion: 120

VEGETABLE CASSEROLE

4 tablespoons olive oil
2 onions, sliced
3 celery sticks, sliced
2 teaspoons ground coriander
2 cloves garlic, crushed
3 carrots, sliced
250 g (8 oz) courgettes, sliced
1 small cauliflower, broken into
florets
1 large potato, cubed
1 × 397 g (14 oz) can tomatoes
1 tablespoon soy sauce
300 ml (1/2 pint) water
salt and pepper
TOPPING:
125 g (4 oz) Cheddar cheese, grated

Heat the oil in a large flameproof casserole, add the onions and celery and fry until softened. Add the coriander and garlic and fry for 1 minute. Add the remaining vegetables, the tomatoes with their juice, soy sauce, water, and salt and pepper to taste. Bring to the boil and stir well. Cover and cook in a preheated moderately hot oven, 190°C (375°F), Gas Mark 5, for 30 minutes, until tender.

Sprinkle with the cheese and place under a preheated hot grill to brown. Serve immediately.

SERVES 6 TO 8
Calories per portion: 200

MONKFISH AMÉRICAINE

3 tablespoons olive oil
2 onions, chopped
750 g (1½ lb) monkfish, cubed
2 cloves garlic, crushed
2 tablespoons wholemeal flour
500 g (1 lb) tomatoes, skinned and
*   chopped*
1 tablespoon tomato purée
120 ml (4 fl oz) white wine
120 ml (4 fl oz) water
bouquet garni
salt and pepper
1 tablespoon chopped parsley

Heat the oil in a pan, add the onions and fry until softened. Add the fish and garlic and fry until golden. Remove and set aside.

Add the flour to the pan, stirring well to mix, then add the tomatoes, tomato purée, wine, water, bouquet garni, and salt and pepper to taste. Bring to the boil, stirring, then simmer, uncovered, for 20 minutes. Return the fish to the pan, cover and simmer for 10 to 15 minutes, until tender.

Remove the bouquet garni. Pour into a warmed serving dish and sprinkle with the parsley.
SERVES 4
Calories per portion: 420

CHICKEN WITH MUSHROOMS

350 g (12 oz) chicken breast fillets
4 tablespoons olive oil
2 onions, sliced
250 g (8 oz) button mushrooms,
*   sliced*
2 tablespoons wholemeal flour
300 ml (½ pint) chicken stock
salt and pepper
2 tablespoons brandy
150 g (5.2 oz) natural yogurt
1 tablespoon chopped parsley

Cut the chicken into 3.5 × 0.5 cm (1½ × ¼ inch) strips. Heat half the oil in a frying pan, add the chicken and fry over high heat, stirring, until sealed. Remove from the pan and set aside.

Heat the remaining oil, add the onions and fry briskly for 2 to 3 minutes, until coloured. Add the mushrooms and cook, stirring, for 1 to 2 minutes. Remove from the heat and stir in the flour. Add the stock and bring to the boil, stirring. Simmer for 2 minutes, then return the chicken to the pan with salt and pepper to taste and cook gently for 5 minutes.

Remove from the heat and pour in the brandy and yogurt. Stir over a low heat until heated through, but do not boil.

Turn into a warmed serving dish and sprinkle with the parsley. Serve with boiled brown rice or a green salad.
SERVES 4
Calories per person: 325

DATE AND APPLE WHIP

750 g (1½ lb) cooking apples,
  peeled and cored
3 tablespoons apple juice
1 teaspoon mixed spice
125 g (4 oz) dates, stoned and
  chopped
1 egg white
2 tablespoons clear honey
120 ml (4 fl oz) natural yogurt
2 tablespoons flaked almonds,
  browned

Slice the apples into a heavy-based pan, add the apple juice and spice, cover and simmer for 10 to 15 minutes. Sieve or work in a blender or food processor until smooth. Turn into a bowl, add the dates and leave to cool.

Whisk the egg white until stiff, then whisk in the honey and continue whisking until very thick. Fold into the apple mixture with the yogurt. Chill until required. Sprinkle with the nuts to serve.

SERVES 6
Calories per portion: 200

STRAWBERRY AND YOGURT CRUNCH

125 g (4 oz) strawberries, sliced
50 g (2 oz) Granola (see page 167)
YOGURT SNOW:
1 egg white
2 tablespoons clear honey
150 g (5.2 oz) natural yogurt

First make the yogurt snow. Whisk the egg white until stiff, then whisk in the honey. Continue whisking until very thick, then carefully fold in the yogurt.

Fold the strawberries into the yogurt snow. Divide half between glasses, sprinkle with Granola, then cover with the remaining yogurt snow. Serve immediately.

SERVES 4
Calories per portion: 140

WATERMELON SORBET

1 × 1.25 kg (2½ lb) watermelon
3 tablespoons clear honey
juice of ½ lemon
1 egg white, stiffly whisked

Scoop out the flesh from the watermelon, discarding the seeds. Place the flesh in an electric blender or food processor with the honey and lemon juice and work until smooth. Pour into a rigid freezerproof container, cover, seal and freeze for 3 to 4 hours, until half frozen.

Turn into a chilled bowl and whisk until fluffy, then gradually whisk in the egg white. Cover, seal and freeze until firm.

Transfer to the refrigerator 15 minutes before serving to soften. Serve in chilled glasses.

SERVES 4
Calories per portion: 100

SUMMER FRUIT SALAD

120 ml (4 fl oz) pineapple juice
1 tablespoon clear honey
125 g (4 oz) strawberries, halved
2 oranges, peeled and segmented
1 banana, sliced
125 g (4 oz) grapes, halved and
  pipped
2 kiwi fruit, peeled and thinly sliced
2 tablespoons kirsch
TO SERVE (OPTIONAL):
1 passion fruit
Yogurt snow (see opposite)

Mix the pineapple juice and honey together in a bowl. Add the fruits and kirsch, mix well and chill for 1 to 2 hours.

Halve the passion fruit, scoop out the flesh and fold into the Yogurt snow. Chill for 1 to 2 hours. Serve with the fruit salad.

SERVES 4
Calories per portion: 200
(without yogurt snow: 130)

INDEX

ACKNOWLEDGMENTS

Photography by Sandra Lousada
Illustrations by Rosalyn Kennedy and Lucy Su
Make-up and hair by Carol Hemming and Christine Skivens
Styling by Alex Anderson
Photographic assistants: Andy Lane, Daphne Wright and Nicola Sutton

The publishers would also like to thank Way In, Harrods and C&A for the loan of the clothes, Stirling Cooper Dance Wear shops for leotards, Fenwicks and Graham and Green for accessories, and Bradleys for lingerie, which were used for photography